HISTORIC CAMEOS

The Key Events In the History of Stratford-upon-Avon

HISTORIC CAMEOS

The Key Events In the History of Stratford-upon-Avon

JOAN McFARLANE

Mayor of Stratford-upon-Avon 1995-1996

Committed to paper by Sarah Summers (Town Clerk)
and Jayne Mottram (Secretary to Joan McFarlane),
ably assisted by Sue Taylor (Office Manager)

C⊕DA
BOOKS LTD

This paperback edition is published in Great Britain in 2017 by

Coda Books Ltd., Office Suite 2, Shrieves Walk, 39 Sheep Street, Stratford-upon-Avon, Warwickshire CV37 6GJ

BOOKS LTD

www.codabooks.com

A CIP catalogue record for this book is available from the British Library.

ISBN: 978-1-9998162-0-9

CONTENTS

VOLUME 5 118

VOLUME 6

- VOLUME 1 -

1. Troughs

In the middle of the 19c approximately 1850, the river water in London and in Stratford-upon-Avon was not clean. The inhabitants of both the city and this town used this water extensively. The Drinking Fountain and Horse Trough Association of London, formed in 1859, loaned Stratford-upon-Avon three troughs, able to take running water, to allow the population and the animals of the town to have fresh water.

One is situated outside the Guild Chapel in Chapel Lane, one at the junction of Sanctus Road and Evesham Road, and one at the entrance to the station at the end of Station Approach.

The name of the lenders is on the side of the Guild Chapel trough and on the other two are the words 'Be merciful to all God's creatures'.

Stratford-upon-Avon has six other troughs given to Stratford-in-Bloom by Miss Elizabeth Creak at the time when she was the first woman to be Chairman of the NFU. These are now filled with flowers twice a year. Miss Creek was High Sheriff in 1988. High Sheriff is the oldest secular office under the crown.

2. The Royal British Legion (29 Bull Street)

The erection of these premises was permitted by Stratford-upon-Avon Borough Council on 22 August, 1925 and the Hon Sec at the time was Mr. R H Rossiter who sought the extension on 25 March 1935; the architect being P W Stowe of 12 Wellesbourne Grove.

Ninety years ago, prior to them arriving in Bull Street in 1925, from July 15 1922, they held their meetings at the Brewery Club, Guild Street. They then moved to the Church of England school on the corner of Grove Road and the Alcester Road which is now the site of a retirement home. In 1928 the Women's Section was formed.

3. The Curfew Bell
The date on the Curfew Bell is 1633 and it is a very heavy bell! It was housed in a gold cupola on the roof of the grand house, which was called Shakespeare Hall and dedicated to Shakespeare, on the corner of Sheep Street and Chapel Street, which subsequently became the Town Hall. The bell probably fell down during the first of the disastrous fires.

Subsequently it became the namesake of the Bell Court Shopping Precinct and was on prominent display. Councillor Juliet Short, in her Mayoral year, rescued it when Bell Court closed, and it is at present in storage with a bell foundry in Newcastle.

4. Important Dates
-   The canal was opened in 1816.
-   The railway 'steel road' arrived in 1859, which opened Stratford-upon-Avon to tourists.
-   Gas arrived in 1843.
-   Sewers were installed in 1850.
-   Electricity came in 1905.

5. Stratford's Royal Charters
Market Charter was given in **1196** by the Bishop of Worcester, the Lord of the Manor, allowing a Thursday street market.

1196 – The Bishop's Charter decreed Borough status allowing the residents to manage themselves (Burgage plots, Burgesses and Bailiffs).

1214 – The Charter given by King John for a three day fair to mark the feast of the Holy Trinity.

1553 – The Charter of Incorporation, Edward VI – local government begins.

1610 – King James Charter allowing the four Chief Officers.

1664 – King Charles II decreed a name change from Bailiff to Mayor.

1674 – King Charles II decreed a Charter to allowed two maces to be carried before the Mayor.

1819 – King George III Charter which changed the Thursday market to a Friday.

1928 – Women allowed to vote, which is the year Stratford-upon-Avon appointed its first lady Mayor, Annie Justins.

1974 – Grant of Arms Charter to the Town Council from the Borough Council.

6. Lighting In the Ballroom of the Town Hall

In 1769 there were seventy pairs of ormolu candlesticks attached to the recoco sconces, given by Garrick. It is thought than none have survived.

In 1818 three handsome cut glass chandeliers, two of six lights and one of ten lights were given by Henry the 6th Barron Middleton who lived at the old Avonbank.

In 1843 the chandeliers were changed to gas at a charge of £28.15s.

In 1934 the same chandeliers were changed to electricity.

7. China In the Ballroom of the Town Hall

On 26 February 1824, five hundred and sixty-two pieces of blue and white china were purchased. There is no makers mark but they were bought from Thomas Dimmock Jnr and Co, a pottery in Shelton in Staffordshire at the cost of £17.8s.6d.

On 8 May the same year, the large pieces were purchased at a cost of £1.16s.6d.

Today, only one hundred and sixty-seven pieces are left following the fire of 1946. Much of it is still on display in the Ballroom.

8. Tea Service

The service was made by Messrs Grainger Lee & Co in 1880. Only sixty-four pieces remain. This is still used on important occasions, including Mayoress' at Home.

Example of the tea service.

9. Transport

The tramway wagon, recently restored by Stratford-on-Avon District Council to pristine condition, and two fire engines were given to the town by the Chairman and Directors of Great Western Railway Company when the rails were taken up in 1916. The rails were going to be used in France to be put in trenches, but failed to cross the channel.

10. Maces

The Guild Verge 1550 – Acquired by the Corporation in 1553. Probably the Verge of the Guild of the Holy Cross. (A verge equals a rod, stick or staff denoting authority).

The Charter Mace 1553 – Dates from the Charter of Incorporation in 1553. Both ceased to be used in 1867. At present they are housed at the Shakespeare Birthplace Trust.

The Sadler Mace 1632 and Quiney Mace – The Sadler Mace was given at the same time as the Quiney Mace by John Sadler and Richard Quiney on 22 August 1632. The Sadler Mace remains in use today. The Quiney mace was broken up in 1757, the value at that time was £8.10s.7 1/2d for thirty-two ounces of gold.

The Ludford Mace was given by John Bracebridge Ludford Esq of Ansley Hall in the county of Warwick. John Ludford was appointed Steward of the Court of Records of the Borough on 24 September 1746. This mace was acquired to replace the discarded Quiney mace.

These maces had to be altered by act of parliament. All maces used in the commonwealth had to be made in the same form and pattern. In 1653/54, Richard

Hunt, who was Bailiff, was reimbursed £19.14s for these alterations. These are now called Royal Maces.

11. The Guild and College Estates

The Guild was brought into being by the growth of the town, for most towns had similar Guilds. It is interesting to speculate why The Guild was dedicated to the Holy Cross. It may be connected with King Richard 'taking the Cross' i.e. going on the crusade to recover Jerusalem and the supposed 'True Cross'.

The Guild had been established before 1269 in the reign of Henry III, and in that year the Bishop of Worcester licenced the Guild to build a chapel and found a hospital for poor priests – which still exists as the Guild Chapel, on the corner of Church Street and Chapel Lane.

The first Master of the Guild was Robert de Stratford who is represented in the centre panel of the beautiful east window of the Guild Chapel, together with his coat of arms. These arms are a modification of those of the Bishop of Worcester, and half way between the arms of the borough (as adopted in 1553) and the Bishop's arms.

The main purpose of the Guild of the Holy Cross was to encourage its members, known as brethren and sistern, to lead a corporate, holy life and also pray and say masses for the souls of dead members.

Members could also enrol their deceased relatives and friends who need not have necessarily lived in the borough. In fact, membership included several members of the Royal family (ref page 13 'History of Local Government in Stratford' by John Winterburn).

The register of the Guild in 1428 mentions that Margaret Lane of Bishopton paid a fine (entrance fee) of

6s 8d and 1lb of corn and 1lb of wax so that she and the soul of her late husband, William, could be received into the fraternity. That meant that masses would be said for them in perpetuity at an altar in the north isle of Holy Trinity Church and their souls would thereby be saved from the dreadful torment of hell, depicted so vividly by the wall painting above the chancel arch in the Guild Chapel.

12. College Estate

John de Stratford, a former rector of Stratford, who subsequently became Bishop of Winchester, enlarged the church at the beginning of 14 century. In 1331 he built and endowed a chancery chapel in the south isle dedicated to Thomas a Beckett. This College required a College of priests to take turns in celebrating masses and five was the regular number of priests in the College.

A little later, in 1353, the nephew of John, Ralph de Stratford, built the College premises to house the priests. It was opposite the church, more or less on the site of the present day Methodist Church. The College became a great land owner in Stratford, and its estates, with those of the Guild, formed the basis of Stratford Corporation's wealth. They still exist today, formally administered by the Borough Council, then the Town Council, and now by Stratford-upon-Avon Town Trust.

The existence of the College is why Holy Trinity Church is described to this day as a Collegiate Church. Exactly the same situation as St Mary's Warwick.

The analogy with Warwick can be pressed further because there was also a Medieval Guild of St George whose premises, the Guild Hall and St James's Chapel are the present Lord Leycester Hospital for retired soldiers. These premises correspond to the Guild Hall and chapel at Stratford, which today are occupied by King Edward VI Grammar School.

13. The Seal and the Arms of the Borough

The Seal of 1553/4 is on loan to the Shakespeare Birthplace Trust, from the Town Council. It is a copper disc, about 2.5 inches in diameter and bares the arms of the borough. It has three leopard heads, two above and one below a chevron and a florid shield. It is mounted on a mulberry wooden handle dated 1865. Florid means a shield with scalloped edges, and was a type of shield much favoured in 16c heraldry.

It originated in Germany and the notches were spear rests, which was very appropriate in Shakespeare's time. The seal was used for stamping wax by means of a vice for impressing parchment or paper. It was replaced by a modern version to the same general design in 1865. Round the edges of the disc are the words 'the seal of the borough town of Stratford' and you can see it on the glass swing doors at the entrance to the Town Hall.

A coloured representation of it in stained glass is in one of the Guild Chapel windows below the figure of Richard Simons, the first Town Clerk (1554-1568). During that time, he lost three children due to the plague.

The origin of the arms of the borough is unknown. What is certain is that the arms on the seal were registered at Warwick during the Herald's Visitation of Warwickshire in 1619. The Heralds returned in 1682 and in the latter case, the Bailiff's seal of the same design was placed on a signet ring, now displayed in the Birthplace.

The colours, or tinctures for the common seal have been various, four different versions are known.

14.   King Richard I (The Lionheart)

King Richard was one of three sons of King Henry II, but also has a sister called Joan. He was also known as Coeurlion even before his accession because of his great reputation as a military leader and warrior. The Saracens called him the King of England, even before he was. He was born on 8 September 1157 in Oxford and died on 6 April 1199. He was 6'5" tall.

Aged 16, Richard was commanding his own army of 8,000 men and he owned 100 ships. He was Central Commander during the third crusade and during that crusade; he tried to recapture Jerusalem against Saladin, his aim being to recover the True Cross.

He spoke only French and lived in South West France with his mother, using his kingdom as a source of revenue. He battled his father, King Henry II, to reign over the territory his father had promised him. He was crowned King in Westminster Abbey on 3 September 1189. He hated England because it was always raining and said that he would 'sell London if he could find someone to sell it to'.

15.   The Legend of the Holy Cross or the True Cross

Seth the son of Adam was given seeds from the 'Tree of Life' by the angel at the gates of paradise and from these rose a tree which was cut down for the building of the great temple by Solomon. The timber in time was acquired by Judas and used for the cross. Judas was forced to show the Empress who was Seth's wife its whereabouts. (The legend is the basis for the wall paintings in the Guild Chapel).

Much artwork on the side walls is covered by oak panelling covering the 'Dance of Death' mural. This mural has four figures in each panel, two figures of death with two victims which equals sixty participants in all. This artwork was under the post reformation declarations.

16. Clopton Bridge

Stratford bridge was, and still is, one of the most important features of the town and is important in its local government history. The original wooden bridge was replaced by the present stone bridge in 1495, which has fourteen arches, two of which were blown up during the Civil War (closest to the Swans Nest Hotel). The bridge was the gift of Sir Hugh Clopton who was Lord Mayor of London. The existence of the bridge helped in the grant of one of The Charters.

There existed a group of volunteers called the 'Bridge Wardens' who held the equivalent of 'bring and buy sales' to raise money for the maintenance of the bridge.

Where villages became towns, two other characteristic developments usually took place. Firstly religious or trade guilds were set up having a corporate life, a common seal and gradually coming to own a great deal of property and exert a great deal of influence.

17. Shrieve's House
(Otherwise Known As 40 Sheep Street)

Before 1549 Stratford was in the manor of the Bishop of Worcester. In 1196 the then Bishop, Bishop de Coutances laid out one hundred and nine acres of his demesne in six streets whose lines remain today. The land was marked out in burgage plots (12 perches by three and a half perches or one hundred and ninety-eight feet by fifty-seven feet nine inches). Shrieve's

House sits on one of these which has remained almost unaltered ever since.

18. The Tudor Bonnet
It is worn as traditional clothing with gowns most especially livery, burgesses and Guilds Officers as suitable head wear.

19. Dressing In the Dark
During this period of abstinence of national street lighting, and having no candles in the house, if you are the proud possessor of Marks & Spencer clothing you can dress in the dark because the label, allegedly, is always on the inside left.

20. Town Wards
In 1850 three electoral wards were formed, Guild Ward, Market Hall Ward and New Town Ward. In 1924 the ward boundaries were revised and Alveston was added as the new fourth ward. This meant there were twenty-seven Councillors and Aldermen (John Winterburn page 44). In 1999, a further revision led to the present day ward names i.e. Alveston, Avenue & New Town, Guild & Hathaway and Mount Pleasant.

The town boundaries are identified as:
- Warwick Road – beyond Evans B&B and before the turning to Snitterfield
- Tiddington Road – just beyond Kissing Tree Lane
- Loxley Road – ends beyond Reg's Romany Caravan
- Banbury Road – beyond Croft Farm
- Shipston Road – beyond Springfield House

- Turning to Clifford Chambers – stream by Clifford Mill
- Severn Meadows Road is the boundary
- Evesham Road – top of Bordon Hill
- Luddington Road – Racecourse
- Alcester Road – roundabout (A46)
- Birmingham Road – roundabout (A46)

21. The Shakespeare Memorial Fountain and Clock Tower

(Affectionately known as the American Fountain)

In 1878 the Dean of Westminster gave a talk in Philadelphia where he mentioned there was no statue in Stratford-upon Avon to commemorate Shakespeare's life. His host was the millionaire newspaper proprietor, George W Childs (1829-1894) who was a very selfless and generous man. Subsequently, he paid for a stained glass window in the chancel in Holy Trinity Church. In 1886 a committee was set up to restore the church, when it was suggested to Mr. Childs that he might like to erect a drinking fountain to cement Anglo American relations, to honour Shakespeare and commemorate Queen Victoria's Golden Jubilee.

The memorial is Victorian Gothic and is made of Peterhead granite and freestone. It is engraved with a number of quotations from Shakespeare's plays. The memorial is situated in Rother Street. 'Rother' is Anglo Saxon for long haired cattle. Its design is based on a Gothic cathedral and the set of bells within were made by Jethro A Cossins of Birmingham.

The fountain consists of three layers. At the corner of the first layer are four pinnacles. At the corners of the second layer are four finials. On the third stage is a tower.

It has four clock faces which are gabled. Above each clock face there is a caricature of a fairy from 'A Midsummer Night's Dream'. The lions and eagles which adorn it represent England and the United States of America and the eagles are holding shields of the Royal Arms and the Stars and Stripes.

Water connection has now ceased but the troughs are filled twice a year by Stratford-in-Bloom. At floor level there are two troughs for smaller animals maintained by the Town Council's Open Spaces team.

22. Gower Memorial

Lord Ronald Charles Sutherland-Leveson-Gower (2 August 1845 – 9 March 1916), who was working on a memorial in France, came to Stratford and stayed with Sir Arthur and Lady Hodgson hoping to become involved with George W Childs' memorial.

In 1887 the Mayor laid the foundation stone. Lord Gower had decided to 'go it alone' on the Bancroft, but attended the unveiling of the Childs' memorial. In 1888 Lord Gower came to unveil his own memorial on the Bancroft.

23. The Court of St James

The Court is named after St James Palace which has always been the official residence of the Sovereign. The Court moved with the present Queen to Buckingham Palace, which is where she wanted to live. In 2009 there were 172 foreign missions which equalled 46 High Commissioners for the Commonwealth and 128 Embassies for the non-Commonwealth countries. All these countries were accredited to the Court of St James in London.

24. Police

The police force in Stratford-upon-Avon comprised a Superintendent with a salary of one pound a week and three night Constables at 10 shillings a week, each. They were provided with 'blue coats'. The day duties were from 6:00am to 10:00pm and the night duties from 10:00pm to 6:00am. In 1889 the police headquarters moved from 1 Sheep Street to Guild Street, where it remained until 1977 when the present police headquarters was built.

25. Alveston Mill

Currently, Access is down Mill Lane and is surrounded by a fence.

The Mill has been in existence since 966. In the Doomsday Survey, there were three mills valued at 40 shillings, 3 sticks and 1,000 eels. This is noted in the Doomsday Book which was compiled in 1081.

In 679 a Monastery was on the site of Holy Trinity Church, or near. In 1240 there were two mills in Tiddington; a corn mill and a fulling mill. All these mills existed until 1650 and they were all in ruins by 1886 and the final one was demolished in the 1940s. Only the Weir remains.

26. The Electric Light Company

Stratford-upon-Avon Electricity Company was registered on 16 November 1905. It was formed to supply power and light to the town centre. The supply commenced on 27 April 1907. At that time the population of Stratford was 9,000. Lighting cost 5 pence per btu and power cost tuppence ha'penny.

DC Electricity was first supplied to the town centre for light from 3 May 1907. A water turbine and generator was on the site of the old Alveston Mill connected by a 6 mile cable to a power house in Arden Street. There was extra current provided for battery charging. On 10 May Stratford Electricity Company invited tenders for condensing plant, switchboard, instruments and electrical connections for a 500KW. The opening of the works was on 3 May 1907 as reported in the Stratford Herald where it was reported that the weather was anything but fine.

There was a main dynamo of 50KW and a second dynamo of 25KW.

Mrs. Coles provided the food for the occasion in a marquee near the station. The Mayor and entourage were in attendance.

The Corporation owned the gas works but was forced to take over the electricity company by outsiders. This was the dictat from the Board of Trade.

The Corporation used to provide the gas for the Town Hall which was installed in 1843 because it was cheaper than electricity, but it was quickly changed to electricity in 1907 because of damage to the fabric and dirty paint work caused by the gaslight.

Businesses had started using their own generators out of necessity one of the first being Frank Organ who owned a furniture business at the end of Cooks Alley. But on 19 October 1904 (Stratford Herald) the town was lit from a central generating station in Rother Street so generators were no longer required.

27. Penicillin

Penicillin is a group of antibiotics derived from Penicillium fungi. Fleming recounted the date of his discovery was on the morning of Friday 28 September,

1928. It was a fortuitous accident in his laboratory in the basement of St Mary's Hospital, London.

Florey, Fleming and Chain shared a Nobel Prize in 1945 for their work on penicillin. Australia was the first country to make the drug available for civilian use, the author of this booklet was one of the first British civilians to be administered with this amazing drug which prevented her left leg from being amputated when she was just eleven years old.

28.   Morris Dancing In Stratford-upon-Avon

Morris dancing has long been a feature of town life. We find in the Chamberlain's Accounts of 29 May, 1717 that the Mayor ordered 5 shillings should be given to the morris dancers. Another 5 shillings was given to them in 1732 to celebrate the Queen's birthday.

Shakespeare was acquainted with the dancing and refers to it in his plays. In Henry V, it is mentioned "busied with A Whitsun morris-dance". He had probably experienced it in the streets of Stratford. There are references to morris dancers performing on Saints' day and being in trouble with the Church court in 1622.

In the last century, the Shakespeare Birthday Celebrations were keen to include morris dancing. As there was no team in the town at the time, a troupe from Bidford-on-Avon was invited in 1904 and 1905. In 1907, a team was especially formed in Stratford to take part (Philip Taylor – 2012).

29.   The National Anthem (2nd Verse!)
O Lord our God arise,
Scatter her enemies

And make them fall;
Confound their politics,
Frustrate their knavish tricks,
On Thee our hopes we fix,
God save us all!

30.   Pollarding

Pollarding enabled farmers to grow crops and tend livestock beneath trees. At the same time, they were able to have a crop of wood from above.

31.   Stratford Leisure Centre

The centre was opened by David Hemery in 1974.

VOLUME 2

32. Stratford's Main Streets (Robert Bearman)

Bridge Street – This street was in existence before the planned town of 1196 was conceived, forming part of the Roman road running down to the ford over the River Avon, with stalls down the middle which led to shops. These were finally demolished in the 1850's. The street was divided by the shops into Fore Street and Back Street.

Wood Street – Was the site of a timber market!

Ely Street – This street was formally known as Swine Street as in 1270 it was described as the street where pigs were sold!

High Street – This street is in the middle of the medieval planned town with two important market areas:

i) The Corn Market at the Town Hall end, which eventually moved into the arcade in the ground floor of the Town Hall. The proper Corn Exchange was built in its place in the 18th Century replacing a town inn called the 'Wheatsheaf'.

ii) The other was at the Market Cross end, the Market Cross stood approximately 8 yards from the door of Barclays Bank.

Windsor Street – This street was previously called Hell Lane, a contraction of Henley Lane.

Henley Street – This street is the only one which departed from the grid pattern on which Stratford-upon-Avon is formed. Presumably it was named such, as it led to Henley-in-Arden.

Meer Street – Is a curved street because it follows the line of a stream which seems to have flowed into the town. It was known as Meer Pool Lane.

Sheep Street – The street where sheep were sold! This street was badly damaged during the disastrous fires of 1594, 1595 and 1614.

Shrieve's House, mentioned in volume one, still bears the scars of a fire on a newel post.

No 31, with its jaunty gable, is a tiny building dating back, supposedly, to the 14th Century and thus is the oldest domestic house still standing, together with Masons Court in Rother Street.

Greenhill Street – The name is very old as in 1260 it was called Grenhulstret (old English), also known as Moor Towns End.

33. Punishment of Rogues and Vagabonds

The Cage – In 1470 it was attached to the outside of a shop on the corner of High Street and Bridge Street, which is now known as Evelyn and Crabtree. It was meant for petty criminals to be humiliated for short periods.

The Pillory – Stood near the Corn Market.

The Whipping Post – Was set up at Market Cross to punish the aforementioned rogues and vagabonds.

34. Banks

HSBC numbers 12 to 13 Chapel Street, is one of the few examples of high Victorian architecture. Established in 1810 it was known as the Olde Bank.

This Bank was 'Oldater Tomes and Chattaway', these names are over the door. There are scenes from Shakespeare's plays running as a frieze around the building below the first floor windows. The building itself is made of red sandstone.

35. The Doomsday Book (Wikipedia)

The Doomsday Book which was written on parchment (prepared sheepskin) is really two independent works:

i) The Little Domesday Book

ii) The Great Domesday Book

Both these books are The Doomsday Book which is held at the National Archives, Kew, in south west London.

It was completed in 1086 and is a record of the great survey of much of England and parts of Wales. It was executed for William I (William the Conqueror). The purpose was to determine who had what and what taxes were liable to be paid.

William was spending Christmas 1085 in Gloucester, where he had discussions with his counsellors. He sent men all over each Shire to find out what each landowner was worth.

In 1179, Richard Fitznigel stated that the book was known by the English as the Domesday Book – that is the 'Day of Judgment'.

The book became unalterable and therefore passed into law.

In 1873, The Return of Ownership of the Land was the forerunner to the Land Registry, which presented the first subsequent picture of the distribution of the land in the British Isles, and is sometimes referred to as the modern Domesday.

In 2006 an online version of the Domesday Book was made available by the United Kingdom National Archives site.

36.   Hedgerows (Subsequently Shortened to Hedges)
In some cases they were remnants from the wildwood from which early fields were created. The fields became common in 1000BC.

The enclosure acts from 1720 to 1840 led to 200,000 miles of hedges being planted. These are known as ancient hedgerows and are protected by law.

118,000 miles have since disappeared since 1950, due to intense farming.

They remain the quintessential feature of the United Kingdom countryside and are also protected by European Law.

37.   York House Hotel
This Hotel, now known as the Stratford-upon-Avon Herald Offices, was the venue for the summer holiday of the family of author, Joan, in 1940, when she was nine years old. Joan, and her sister, shared a room overlooking the Shakespeare Memorial Fountain and Clock Tower, which is now the editor's office.

38.   A Royal Charter
Is a document to establish a new body or trust and sets out its powers and responsibilities. It is granted by the Queen and cannot be altered by Parliament. A good example of a Royal Charter is the Charter Mop Fair.

39.   The Guild and College Estates
(Richard Eggington, 2013)
On a cool damp evening in July 1999, the elected members of Stratford Town Council gathered at the Town Hall for a meeting that would be of monumental significance in the civic history of the town. In attendance was a

strong delegation from the Charity Commission, who was to deliver its verdict on the Council's management of these two ancient charitable trusts.

The Council had managed the Charities in the same way that its predecessors had for hundreds of years. It was aware that the Commission, during months of enquiry, had identified things that needed to be changed. The Council was willing to oblige.

When the head of the Commission's team rose to announce their conclusions, the news was devastating. The Charity Commission was not prepared to sanction the continued trusteeship of the Charities by the Town Council. This resulted in the formation of Stratford-upon-Avon Town Trust.

40. The Third Verse of the National Anthem
This was always thought to be the second – there are five verses in all.

> *Thy choicest gifts in store*
> *One her be pleased to pour*
> *Long may she reign*
> *May she defend our laws*
> *And ever give us cause*
> *To sing with heart and voice*
> *God Save the Queen*

41. Before or After
Should one put milk in the cup before or after pouring tea (pre or post lactic)? This is a question that can destroy a good dinner party!

The definitive answer is in a book called 'Creating a Stir – 125 years of Tea' by S D Bell, owner of a Belfast

Teahouse. The Bell family were friends of the author and her family during their time of residence in Belfast from 1963-1966.

Milk should be put in the cup first as milk is a colloid, a liquid whose elements are not chemically connected and can easily be separated. This separation occurs easily when it is poured into hot tea after the tea has been poured.

42.   The Curfew Bell *(Mentioned in Volume 1)*
The Curfew Bell was rung during the reigns of William I and II at sunset, to give notice that their subjects were to extinguish fires and candles. (French… *'couvre-feu'* – 'cover the fire'). It was later adapted into Middle English as 'curfeu', and later still, into the modern 'curfew'.

Subsequently the curfew has been used to maintain law and order.

43.   Stratfords of the World (Formerly Sister Cities)
Stratford-upon-Avon forged a friendly association with Stratford Ontario in the early 1980's.

In 1984, Connecticut High School Band travelled to Ontario to give concerts in several of their schools and churches.

In the spring of 1985, the Connecticut School Band toured England. During this visit, long lasting links with Stratford-upon- Avon were established.

In 1987, Stratford-upon-Avon hosted both the Connecticut and Ontario bands. This was the time when the Sister Cities relationship was put on a formal footing. The Sister Cities concept began during Edward Lloyd's Mayoralty.

From 1995, the visits became biannual and the subsequent host was chosen at the end of each visit.

In 2013, the relationship stands at six Stratford's globally: Connecticut, Ontario, Prince Edward Island, England, New Zealand and Australia.

44. Cathedral (From the Greek Meaning Seat)
A cathedral is a Christian church which contains the seat of a Bishop. A town can only be called a city if it contains such a seat; thus, only cathedral towns become cities.

There are sixty-six cities in the United Kingdom. Any town can apply to the Crown to become a city, and during the Queen's Diamond Jubilee in 2012, Perth in Scotland, Chelmsford in England and St Asaph in Wales were all granted city status by the Monarch, Queen Elizabeth II.

In the ancient world, the 'chair' was a symbol of a teacher, and then of a bishop's role as a teacher. It, therefore, became a major symbol of authority.

45. The Swan Fountain
In order to commemorate the 800th anniversary of the town in 1995, town residents were invited to put forward ideas.

The Swan Fountain was the idea of a Bridgetown resident, who put it before the incumbent Mayor, Cllr Joan McFarlane. After approval by the Town Council, a competition for the design ensued which was won by sculptor, Mrs. Christine Lee. Architect, Mr. Roger Abbott, was commissioned. Sponsorship was sought and obtained from Country Artists of Stratford-upon-Avon.

It was constructed by a local company, and installed in a circular basin on the Bancroft Gardens, directly opposite the bottom of Sheep Street. During the refurbishment of the Gardens, it was subsequently moved slightly and the circular basin was changed.

The following year, on Friday 18 November 1996, the Mayor, Cllr Charles Bates and Town Councillors, were delighted to welcome HM the Queen, who switched it on. Her Majesty, accompanied by the Duke of Edinburgh, arrived in a beautiful, new, maroon Bentley. They took tea with the Town Council in the Ballroom. A special cake was baked, which her Majesty had difficulty cutting with a sword!

Thereafter, the Royal couple visited the Guild Chapel.

46. The Cemetery

The Town Council is the burial authority for the town, and the Cemetery is managed by the Town Council's Open Spaces team, currently headed by Tony Holt, who has served over twenty-five years with the Council. He, and his team, also manage Holy Trinity Churchyard, the Alveston Memorial, the Remembrance Garden and the Town Council's allotments.

Some graves within the Cemetery are three coffins deep, but this practice is no longer followed, the depth is limited to two coffins, plus cremated internments. If hand dug, a grave can take up to three days to excavate but as long as the weather is kind, a mechanical digger is used. Re-openers are, however, still dug by hand.

47. The High Steward

The High Steward is an honorary title bestowed by the councils or charter trustees of certain towns and cities in England. Originally, it was a judicial office with considerable local powers. By the 17th Century it had declined to a largely ceremonial role.

Sir William Dugdale who lives some way north of the town is the current incumbent. The title is usually awarded for life.

48. The Lord Lieutenant (Wikipedia)

The title Lord Lieutenant is given to the British Monarch's personal representative in the United Kingdom, usually a county or similar circumscription, with varying tasks throughout history. Usually a retired local notable, senior military officer, peer or businessman is given the post honorarily. Both men and women are eligible for the post.

The main duties are:

- Arranging visits of the Royal Family;
- Escorting Royal visitors;
- Presenting medals on behalf of the Sovereign;
- Advising on honours nominations;
- Participating in civic, voluntary and social activities within the Lieutenancy.

The appointment is for life, although the customary age for retirement is 75.

Warwickshire underwent a change in March 2013; Sir Martin Dunne was succeeded by Mr. Timothy Cox, following Sir Martin's retirement.

49. High Sheriff (Wikipedia)

The High Sheriff is the oldest, secular office under the Crown.

He, or she, is a legal officer with an unpaid ceremonial role within the county, and appointed annually by the crown. Principal responsibilities include attendance at

Royal visits and opening ceremonies when a High Court Judge goes on the circuit.

The earliest record the author can find is:

Alwin in 1066;

1585 – Anthony Shuckburgh of Shuckburgh Hall;

1857 – Henry Spencer Lucy of Charlecote House;

1971 – Captain Sir William Dugdale of Blyth Hall;

1973 – Captain George West of Alscot Park;

1976 – Sir John Wiggin of Honington Hall;

1979 – George Docker of Alveston;

1981 – Sir Dennis Flower of Ilmington;

1982 – Sir Martin Dunne of Radway;

1988 – Miss Elizabeth Creak of Stratford on Avon;

2003 – Sir William Dugdale of Blyth Hall;

2011 – Mr. Timothy Cox, who later became Lord Lieutenant of Warwickshire in 2012;

2013 – Mr. Keith Sach, the current incumbent.

Each subsequent High Sheriff is chosen by the Queen during the 'Pricking Ceremony'. Although the High Sheriff appointment is pre-arranged, the name of the chosen one is ceremoniously determined when the Queen pierces a sheet of parchment with a bodkin to prevent any tampering.

50.   Hospitals In Stratford-upon-Avon
(Marie MacDonald, 2013)

The first 'modern' hospital in Stratford was in 1823, and was a dispensary. It was run by local doctors for the poor and funded by prescription. Worthy patients were given a voucher for treatment. Originally located in a house in Chapel Street, it moved to a larger premise in Chapel Lane in 1826. The building still survives and is used as administrative offices for the RSC.

In 1861, the dispensary was being called Stratford-upon-Avon Hospital and in 1884, a new purpose built hospital was erected on land between the Alcester Road and Arden Street. The hospital continues today on an adjacent site but with much reduced services.

There were several other specialised hospitals during the 19th and 20th centuries. An isolation hospital was situated at the far end of the Alcester Road before being relocated in 1899 on Avenue Farm, off the Birmingham Road. This was known as the Infectious Disease Hospital and later known as the Isolation Hospital.

The Nursing Institute and Convalescent Home operated in Tyler Street between 1872 and 1876, at which date it moved to numbers 14 to 15 Rother Street, the building currently known as the Civic Hall.

It was renamed the Nursing Home and Children's Hospital. It was the project of the same benevolent family, the Gibbins of Ettington, who were later to endow the new hospital on the Alcester Road. This was later known as the Stratford-upon-Avon Convalescent Home and District Nursing Institution.

During the Second World War, it served as a maternity home for women evacuated from bombed areas, especially Coventry. When this closed after the war, the isolation hospital became the Children's Recovery Hospital, remaining so until its closure in 1973.

51. The Solstices and the Equinox

The summer and the winter solstices occur in June and December when the sun is at its greatest distance from the equator. 'Sol' equals 'sun' and 'sistere' equals 'to cause to stand still'.

The vernal and the autumnal equinox occur when the day and the night are of equal length.

52. Tea (Camellia Sinensis)

Tea, or tcha, in Chinese, is known in common English as char.

In the 17th century, tea was only grown and drunk in China. Budhists were the first to cultivate the tea tree, which grew below a mountain on the slopes above a river close to Shanghai. Tea was considered to be a medicine and was only sold in an apothecary. It was very expensive, which only the rich could afford. Because of this, it was locked away in a Tantalus.

London eventually became the centre of the international tea trade. The Cutty Sark is an example of a tea clipper.

Assam, part of India, was the next part of the world from which England obtained their tea; the tea trees having being transplanted there.

Baraset House in Tiddington owned by the late Mr. Percy Swiffen was the name of his tea plantation in India about 15 miles from Calcutta.

The tea plantation houses were called bungalows. They were low houses on stilts to allow the plantation workers, who were riding elephants, to walk along side and alight at the level of the living quarters.

In 1888, India overtook China in the provision of tea for the English market. Calcutta was the epicentre.

There is nothing more quintessentially English than drinking tea. The only tea plantation in England, Tregothnan Estate, is near Truro in Cornwall. The Estate, has been the home of the Boscawen family since 1335. The family named Bergamot flavoured Earl Grey tea after an ancestor, Charles Grey, who was Prime Minister in the early 19th century.

53. Shakespeare's Baptism and Burial

Shakespeare's Baptism was noted in Holy Trinity Church in Latin. His burial was noted in English followed by the word "Gent" which meant he was entitled to a Coat of Arms (Arms emblazoned on armour), hence "Call to arms" in battle.

54. David Garrick

David Garrick, the famous actor, led tourism to Stratford-upon- Avon by starting a three day Jubilee in 1769. He gave a statue for the newly built Town Hall, which can still be seen in a niche on the north wall. There is a maquette of it in the Town Council's collection of artifacts.

The actor was granted the Freedom of the Borough.

55. Marie Corelli (Wikipedia)

Marie Corelli was a British novelist, who sold more copies of her books than her contemporaries, Conan Doyle, H G Wells and Rudyard Kipling put together.

Born, Mary Mackay, in London on 1 May 1855, she was the illegitimate daughter of a Scottish poet and songwriter and his servant, Elizabeth Mills.

In 1866, eleven year old Mary was sent to a Parisian Convent to complete her education.

Marie lived with her companion, Bertha Vyver, for over 40 years in her house in Church Street known as Mason Croft, is now the home of the Shakespeare Institute.

She was instrumental in the preservation of Stratford's 17th century Buildings, and donated money to help remove the plaster or brickwork that often covered there facades; a good example being the Falcon Hotel.

Marie was responsible for saving the Henley Street public library, as the Shakespeare Trust wanted to sell the five cottages standing there, which once belonged to the Shakespeare family.

Known to be eccentric, Marie could be seen driving around Stratford in a carriage pulled by miniature black ponies and owned a gondola on the river complete with an imported Italian gondolier, who was later sent home for being drunk.

She spent her final years in Stratford-upon-Avon until her death on 21 April 1924, and is buried in the Stratford-upon-Avon Cemetery on Evesham Road.

56. Fourth Verse of the National Anthem
(One to Go)

Not in this land alone
But be God's mercies known
From shore to shore
Lord make the matrons see
That men should brothers be
And form one family
The wide world over.

57. Elgin Gardens (Tiddington Road)
The field on this prestigious road used to be known, affectionately, as the Donkey Field.

The name 'Duncan', is derived from the word 'Donkey' – brown haired, and Duncan I of Scotland was killed by Macbeth at Elgin on the 15th August 1040.

The Parish Council, which has the prerogative of naming new roads, chose 'Elgin' to make it easier for postal workers and residents alike.

58. The Toll House
(The Stratford Society and Maurice Ribbans)

Built in 1814, it was used to collect tolls from horse drawn coaches and wagons, horse riders, cattle and sheep which were driven across the bridge (Maurice Ribbans, page 20).

It has a four centred head and a door of four arched panels.

The life of the Toll House was short lived, because in 1816, its roof was reported to be in poor repair and the riverbank unsafe. One bridge user is recorded as putting his foot through one of the Toll House windows in protest at paying. In 1839 the levy came to an end.

On 7th May 2013, scaffolding was seen to be erected on the river side of the Toll House. Who knows what will become of it now, but it is work in progress for the newly constituted Heritage Buildings Trust.

59. The Swan's Nest Hotel

The site originally belonged to the family of Sir Hugh Clopton, and the inn started life as 'The Bear', in 1662. After enlargement of the main house, it became a warehouse and then reopened as 'The Shoulder of Mutton'. Its present name is fairly recent.

60. King Henry VIII

King Henry VIII, who was born in 1485 and died in 1547, is most famous for his six wives. He broke from

Rome and became the inadvertent founder of the Church of England, due the need for a son and heir, and his carnal desire for Ann Boleyn.

There is an easy to remember rhyme which charts the fate of his six wives; 'divorced, beheaded, died, divorced, beheaded, survived'.

Catherine of Aragon – marriage annulled

Ann Boleyn – executed

Jane Seymour – died in childbirth

Anne of Cleves – marriage annulled

Catherine Howard – executed

Catherine Parr – widowed

Closer to home, the Lord of the Manor of Henley-in-Arden reverted to the Crown between 1478-1547 and during that time Henry VIII was Lord of the Manor. When he died, the Earl of Warwick succeeded him as Lord of the Manor of Henley-in-Arden.

61. The Bandstand

The original, made of wood, stood outside the main entrance to The Royal Shakespeare Theatre.

The present bandstand, now maintained by Stratford-upon-Avon Town Trust, was fabricated by The Royal Engineers at their base in Long Marston, and was commissioned by the Town Council during the Mayoralty of Stephen Turner in 1994-1995. It was officially opened by the author, Joan McFarlane, during her Mayoral year. A commemorative stone and a plaque on the base, mark these occasions.

62. Masons Court

Was built in Rother Street in 1485. It is said to be the oldest occupied house in Stratford-upon-Avon.

63. 'Under Your Husband's Thumb'
In Shakespeare's time, a husband could beat his wife, if she disobeyed him by not dousing the fire at the *'couvre-feu'* (curfew) with a stick no thicker than his thumb, hence "under your husband's thumb".

64. Shottery Manor (Wikipedia)
Parts of Shottery Manor (the present Stratford-upon-Avon Grammar School for Girls) dates from the 14th century. In the attic of the Manor is a priest hole to the right of the staircase. Legend has it that Shakespeare was betrothed to Anne Hathaway in the chapel, which is now the geography room.

64.1. Tunnels
A secret passage from behind the geography room fireplace led to Sheep Street (questionable!). It is true, however, that a passage exists. This passage is temporarily unblocked and sealed again when it is inspected annually by the Fire Service.

Another passage, five miles long, leads into the country (again, questionable) but there are definitely two tunnels.

65. The Fifth and Last Verse of the National Anthem
In September 1745 the young pretender to the British throne, Prince Charles Edward Stuart, defeated the army of King George II at Prestonpans near Edinburgh. 'God Save the King' was a patriotic song first publicly performed in London in the same year, 1745, which became known as the National Anthem in the 19th century.

The words and tune are anonymous and may date back to the 16 century. In a fit of patriotic fervour, after the Battle of Prestonpans, Scotland, the leader of the band of the Theatre Royal, Drury Lane, arranged for 'God Save the King' to be performed after the play. The practice spread to other theatres in London and the custom of greeting the Monarch with this song was established.

From every latent foe,
From the assassin's blow,
God Save the Queen.
O'er her thine arm extend,
For Britain's sake defend,
Our mother, prince and friend,
God Save the Queen.

VOLUME 3

66.   The Rose and Crown (Sheep Street)

The original Rose and Crown was situated at No 1 Sheep Street next to the Town Hall and is mentioned in Wheeler's History as one of the town's principal inns. It was, in the late eighteen fifties, that the original hostelry closed and the name transferred to an inn on the present site, initially known as The Green Dragon.

Records for the present property do not go back beyond 1596, when a major fire burnt down many of the Sheep Street properties. By 1703 there was a malt house on the site. It was owned by Richard Hull. As The Green Dragon, in 1792, John Hobbies sold it to Edward Payne. In 1858 his son Edmund, inherited it, when at least half of it was named The Rose and Crown as it is known today.

67.   The Stratford Canal

The Stratford Canal is 25 miles long and on 26th April 1958, Stratford Town Hall was crammed with 400 people protesting about the abandonment of the canal. The meeting resolved that somehow the canal must be saved.

The canal played an important part in the transport revolution 200 years ago. In 1964, the canal reopened.

Behind this venture was David Hutchings, who almost single-handedly completed the impossible task of dredging and building the numerous locks, using National Trust staff and volunteers, service personnel and offenders from local jails. Restoration took from

1961 to 1964. David was local Chairman of the England Waterways Association. (He sought planning permission after the task was completed!).

The Stratford Canal begins in Kings Norton where there is a unique, newly restored, guillotine lock.

The canal is fed from the tributary of the River Blythe into Earlswood Lakes which are man-made. There are 25 acres of lakes, namely Engine Pool, Windmill Pool and Terry's Pool.

68. Street Pastors (Google)

Street Pastors was pioneered in London in 2003 by Les Isaac. On that first night, 18 volunteers took to the streets of Brixton, 15 women and three men. 12,000 Street Pastors are now trained to play an active part in 270 towns and cities around the United Kingdom. Street Pastors engage with people on the streets, to care for them, listen to them and help them. They work together with other partners in the night time economy to make amenities safer. Each city project is set up by Ascension Trust, which is the governing body behind Street Pastors and is run by a local coordinator, with support from local churches and community groups, in partnership with the police, local councils and other statutory agencies.

Stratford-upon-Avon Street Pastors aim to be a visible Christian presence on the streets of Stratford-upon-Avon, with the night time economy. Demonstrating the love of Christ by bridge building, offering a helping hand and a listening ear to everyone they meet. The Pastors patrol from 8.30 p.m. to 3.30 a.m. on a Friday or Saturday night. Practical help is given in the form of flip flops and foil blankets as well as their famous lollipops.

69.   Hathaway Tea Rooms

Situated at No 19 High Street, the Hathaway Tea Rooms building is a Grade II listed building and occupies one of the town's most historic sites. The building was constructed around 1610, exactly at the same time as Shakespeare moved into his retirement home, of New Place, on Chapel Street. In 1728, the property was known locally as the George Inn and was owned by Daniel Yeates of Hampton Lovett, who purchased No 19 and No 20 High Street for £160. In 1738, the ownership was passed to Thomas Pasham, a bookseller.

From 1803, the property took on a medical role, first becoming an apothecary, which was an early form of pharmacy and from 1757, became a combined surgery and apothecary in the names of William Smith, Richard Walls, John Knottesford, Thomas Nott and Thomas Mills. From the mid-19th century, it was operated by a boot and shoe manufacturer and it remained a thriving shoe shop until the early nineteen hundreds. Arthur William Rider, possibly the owner's son, is listed as a boarder at King Edward VI school in Stratford between 1886 and 1889. Finally, in 1931, the property became known as the Hathaway Tea rooms and is now run by Rick Allen.

70.   The First Parliament Held In Westminster Hall

The House of Westminster is the meeting place of the House of Commons and the House of Lords, the two houses of the Parliament of the United Kingdom. Commonly known as the Houses of Parliament after its tenants. The Palace lies on the Middlesex Bank of the River Thames in the City of Westminster, in central London. Its name, which derives from neighbouring

Westminster Abbey, may refer to either of the two structures: the old Palace, a medieval building complex, that was destroyed by fire in 1834 and its replacement new Palace, that stands today. For ceremonial purposes, the Palace retains its original style and status as a Royal Residence. The first Royal Palace was built on the site in the 11th century, and Westminster was the primary London residence of the Kings of England until a fire destroyed much of the complex in 1512. After that, it served as the home of Parliament which has been meeting there since the 13th century and the seat of the Royal Courts of Justice, based in and around Westminster Hall. In 1834, an even greater fire ravaged the heavily rebuilt Houses of Parliament, and the only structures of significance to survive, were Westminster Hall, the Cloisters of St Stephen's, the Chapel of St Mary Undercroft and the Jewel Tower.

The first Parliament sat at the House of Westminster on 20th January 1265. 2015 was the 750th anniversary of the first meeting of the House of Commons.

71. Anne Hathaway
(Pitchfork Productions and Shakespeare Birthplace Trust)

Anne Hathaway was born in 1556 and lived in Shottery. She strolled frequently into Stratford. It is possible that she might have met a young William on such a stroll. Anne shared the house with her brother, following the death of both her parents. In those days girls married earlier, as did Anne. Anne found she was pregnant in 1582 and married soon afterwards, which was probably a Catholic service. Anne was 26 and was streetwise, but William, a troubled youth, following the collapse of his father's business, lived in uncertain times.

Anne was devoted to her children and was stricken when the only son, Hamnet, died of an unknown cause in August 1596. Anne's love and encouragement were enough to sow the seeds of ambition in the poet, the inspiration and nature that he needed. Anne died in 1623, having lived just long enough to see a memorial built to her husband in Holy Trinity Church. She is buried in the church, next to him.

72. Marie Corelli *(See also Index No. 55)*
Marie Corelli was born on 1 May 1855 and she died on 21 April 1924. Marie Corelli was a British novelist. She sold more copies than her contemporaries, i.e. Conan Doyle, H G Wells and Rudyard Kipling, all put together.

Marie Corelli and her pet dog

Marie Corelli in her gondola "The Dream" on the Avon.

Mary MacKay (her birth name) was born in London. She was the illegitimate child of a Scottish poet and songwriter, with his servant, Elizabeth Mills. In 1866, 11 year old Mary was sent to a Parisian convent to complete her education.

Marie lived with her companion, Bertha Vyver, for over 40 years in Stratford. She spent her final years here and was known to be very eccentric. Her eccentricity meant that being only short in stature, she would not be photographed unless standing on a box. She was driven round Stratford in a small pony cart pulled by six Shetland ponies. She had a gondola on the river, propelled by a real Italian gondolier, who was subsequently sent home because he was continually drunk. She was instrumental in saving Stratford Library in Henley Street.

She was also instrumental in saving other Stratford 17th century buildings and donated money to help the owners remove the plaster on the brickwork that often covered their facades.

She died in Stratford and is buried in the Evesham Road Cemetery. Her house in Church Street, Mason Croft, is now the home of the Shakespeare Institute.

73. Harvard House

Harvard House was built in 1596 by a wealthy townsman, Alderman Thomas Rogers, who had twice served as High Bailiff. He was a butcher by trade. His initials are carved on the front of the house (with the Bulls Head to denote his trade), together with his wife and eldest son William. The date is 1596. The fires in 1594 and 1595, caused considerable damage to this part of town and was the reason that this house was partly rebuilt. The elaborately carved façade is by far the richest in the town and is testimony to Rogers' wealth and standing.

In the 17th century the house was sold to the Capp family. John Capp, a blacksmith, made alterations.

Two pictures of Harvard House.

He remained in the house until 1755, when the house belonged to a bookseller, a plumber and a series of ironmongers, until 1801.

Thomas and Harvey Williams, breeches makers, owned it until 1871, when it became an estate agent's office. In 1901, after enthusiastic support from Marie Corelli, the freehold was bought by Edward Morris of Chicago. After restoration, it was given to Harvard University. The link with Harvard, dates from 1605 and the marriage in Stratford, of Catherine, daughter of Thomas Rogers who built the house and Robert Harvard of Southwark, also a butcher. The son of this union, John, born in 1607, emigrated to America in 1637. He died a year later and left part of his estate to found a college at Cambridge, Massachusetts, named after him in 1639, Harvard University.

74.   The Toll House, Clopton Bridge
(See also Index No. 58)
(Maurice Ribbans)

This is a ten sided building built in 1814 with a lower ground floor and ground floor. It was used to collect tolls from horse drawn coaches, wagons, horse riders, cattle and sheep. It has a four centred head and a door of four arched panels.

Life for the Toll House was short lived because in 1816, its roof was reported to be in poor repair and the river bank unsafe. One bridge user is recorded as putting his foot through one of its windows, at protest at paying the toll. In 1839, the levy came to an end.

The Heritage Buildings Trust is fully constituted and work begins soon on this fascinating building, to restore this ancient monument.

The Toll House.

It is built of brick walls with stone ashlar facing. In December 1814, an upper floor was added. It was listed Grade I in 1951, in conjunction with the Clopton bridge, which is also a Scheduled Ancient Monument. The roof was described in 1814 as being of elm with Welsh slate finish (indicating a pitched roof). It was then raised in December 1814 with the same roof make up, but apparently poorly built as it was in disrepair by 1816. The tolls ceased by 1840 and the building was rented out as a domestic house.

In 1841, there were seven residents. By 1846, some of the Toll House chimneys had been dismantled and the building converted to use as an office for the timber yard run by James Cox. In 1997 Cox's Yard timber business closed and the Cox's Yard entertainment complex opened. The Toll House was closed and left unused and semi-derelict. The building was in the ownership of Stratford on Avon District Council. In 2007, the Stratford Society undertook some stone repairs, removed the remaining chimney and maintained the building watertight with a temporary felt roof. It is not known when the upper floor was removed.

75. Lucy's Mill Bridge

The first bridge to be built on this site was in 1590. It was paid for by voluntary contributions. It was a wooden structure of seven arches, supported by six large stone piers. In 1618, the corporation adopted the bridge and undertook to keep it in good repair. Extensive repairs were carried out in 1812 and 1827. The passage was widened at the request of the Avon Navigation Company by the removal of one pier, to allow barges to pass. In 1867, a flood destroyed two piers and the bridge had to be completely rebuilt. Finally, in 1934, the rather handsome, wooden bridge was replaced by an art deco bridge of reinforced concrete, to match the art deco of the Shakespeare Memorial Theatre, that had opened two years previously in 1932.

In 2014, the once handsome, art deco bridge was in need of help and following a meeting of approximately 200 people in the Town Hall, a committee was formed to try and rectify the situation.

76. The Firs Garden

In 1910, Marie Corelli, the famous novelist, bought it. The Firs, a nearby house, no longer in existence, lends the garden its name. When it was sold in 1910, Marie Corelli bought the gardens to preserve them as an open space for the benefit of the town.

77. The Guild Chapel

(Historic Spine – Robert Bearman and Paul Burley)

One of the most important groups of buildings in Stratford are those associated with the medieval Guild of the Holy Cross, the most striking of which is its chapel. This dates back to 1269, when the Guild was licensed to build a hospital on this site, with a small chapel attached. Parts of the present chancel, in particular its south wall, may date back to this time. Later the whole building was taken over by the Guild for its own use and in the 1450s the chancel largely rebuilt to provide better facilities for the priests who were engaged to pray for the souls of the Guild's departed members. Then, in the 1490s, Hugh Clopton left money in his will for a grand rebuilding of the nave and west tower. The interior was decorated with a series of elaborate wall paintings, some of which can still be seen.

The Guild Chapel.

The Guild was suppressed at the Reformation and all its property in the town confiscated by the Crown. This, including the chapel, was given back to the newly-established Stratford Corporation in 1553, who at first allowed the chapel to stand empty. In the 1560s, however, it was refurbished as a suitable venue for an increasing number of visiting preachers. This was probably when the old wall paintings were whitewashed over, and any other evidence of the old catholic faith removed. Significant traces of these paintings were rediscovered during restoration work in 1804, including the dramatic portrayal of the Day of Judgment over the chancel arch. From the 1960s, an ongoing programme of restoration has ensured the building's future as a nondenominational place of worship.

A new organ, costing a quarter of million pounds, was installed in 2014 by Stratford Town Trust, who now manage the Guild and College Estates.

78. The Avon Bowling Club
(Opposite Holy Trinity Church)

The bowls have been traced with certainty, to the 13th century. Stones, as it was called, with a Jack or Kitty, was called Casting of Stones. One bowl only was used in the 13th century. The oldest bowling club, was recorded in Southampton, in 1299 on the old bowling green.

It was forbidden in Edward III and Richard II's reigns, as it might jeopardise the practice of archery. The word 'bowls' is first used in King Henry VIII's reign and it was only allowed to be played at Christmas.

A Stratford Herald pamphlet by Charles Clifton and introduced by George Lea, a member of Stratford-upon-Avon Bowling Club, was used for the following research: Early records show that the first bowling green in Stratford was on the Gild Pitts and it was behind the Red Horse Inn. It was called the Green at the Red Horse and was used in very early times.

The Colbourne family handed down the story that it had been played on for between 200 and 400 years (quote). This family owned the Red Horse Hotel, to which The Green belonged. The worthies of the town were involved, including Messrs Bird, Winter and Pearce (all former mayors), as well as Thomas Hunt and Robert Lunn, both town clerks. Other names mentioned are Canning, Randall and F Gibbs.

The Green fell into disuse during World War I but was played on from 1919 and was disposed of in 1932.

Without the enthusiasm of the aforementioned men and their practical help, the present club might never have existed. Records show that J H Rowe (incumbent mayor) presided at an early meeting, attended by many well known names and guarantor was George Lea.

Harry Tossell, who was the manager of the Royal Shakespeare Theatre at the time, was a kind and helpful intermediary, during negotiations for leasing the present Green from the Theatre governors.

In its present position in Southern Lane, the presidents of the club at the time were Alderman J H Rowe, 1934-35 and Alderman George Lea, 1946-52. Both these gentlemen were successful farmers as well as directors of the racecourse. Alderman Rowe was not fond of playing, but Alderman Lea was and played in 100 county matches as their skip.

Councillor R J Knight was the vice president and honorary secretary for 11 years. He was mayor from 1951 to 1952.

The honorary secretary, Fred Archer, for the first three years of the club's existence, 1934-1936, presented a handsome scoreboard in 1955. The honorary treasurer was Tam Horsewell until Southern Lane was firmly established. The first captain was Francis Harris, 1934-35.

The lady in charge of all the catering until 1939, was a Mrs H B Walters. The Green was fashioned by Pat Haylock in an idyllic setting.

To commemorate the Queen's Silver Jubilee on the 6th June 1957, the president presented a handsome pair of gates, gifted by John Leeson, embellished with the borough crest.

In October 1932, they held their first annual dinner at the Falcon and the tickets were three and sixpence each. The mayor elect at the time was Councillor Eleanor Waldron.

The first minute book. A committee meeting was held on the Green in Guild Street on 19 May 1933. Discussion was on the formation of the new green proposed by Mr Walters and the proposition carried was that the groundsman be paid an extra 10 shillings a week, whilst he was attending both greens.

The next committee meeting was held at the Seven Stars on 14th August 1933 and the discussion was about a letter, read from the governors of the Memorial Theatre and their offer, which was the use of a shed at the annual rent of £10 a year. This was accepted. The level of the green was discussed on 24th August in the same year and it was agreed to relay the green after the season was over.

At the committee meeting at the Seven Stars on 26 January 1934, there were five items on the agenda:

1) Mr Louth presented the lease of the green and building, and the money owed was paid.

2) It was proposed that the groundsman and boys be engaged and that the groundsman's wage be not more than 25 shillings a week.

3) It was proposed that furniture be purchased.

4) It was proposed that an AGM at the Seven Stars should be held on 28th February 1934, with a notice in the Stratford Herald.

5) Monthly meetings from then onwards would be held on the first Wednesday of each month.

On 13th August 1934, an alcohol licence was applied for. A Mr Amphlett wrote a letter of complaint and subsequently, he was asked to resign and return his subscription. Mr C A Rookes was thanked for 12 bottles of port.

AGM (allegedly 28th February 1934).

1) It was proposed by Mr Mason and Mr Knight that no boys should be employed on the green. This was carried.

2) It was proposed that ladies should be able to join. The committee was then given powers to decide.

On 5th September 1934, it was proposed that there should be one spiked roller, eight baskets of seed and that the men offered by Mr Evans of Stratford Golf Club, be employed.

On 5th June 1935 it was proposed that an old well on the site should be opened and that two large water tanks be acquired.

On 7th February 1936 at the Seven Stars, it was proposed that an Atco lawn mower be purchased and Colonel Warner was thanked for a pair of goblets to be played for. Thirdly, that two pairs of woods from now on, must be used (formerly only one pair was used).

Mr Henry Tossell of Shakespeare Memorial Theatre, on 4th May 1934, was offered honorary membership because of his kindness and helpfulness to the club.

In 1966, a new flag for the club was given by Harry Boston.

79. The Everyman Statue (Sheep Street)

A statue of a young man in medieval dress, supporting a shield. His stance is casual and he is depicted in a simplified and elongated manner, wearing sandals, tunic, trousers and a cloak. The cloak is tattered and torn, perhaps as if in battle, or perhaps reflecting his lowly position as a servant.

The Everyman Statue.

The shield is that of the former Stratford Borough. After the local government reorganisation of 1974, the arms of the former Stratford Borough were transferred by the Earl Marshal to Stratford-upon-Avon Town Council.

The statue was commissioned as part of the building in 1964 and is commonly believed to represent the idea of 'everyman'.

In literature and drama, the term everyman has come to mean an ordinary individual, with whom the audience or reader is supposed to be able to identify easily, and who is often placed in extraordinary circumstances. The name derives from a 16th century English morality play called Everyman.

80. Alveston
(Further information following on from Vol. 2)
Alveston's original name was Eanulfestun and was the homestead of Eanulf, its tenant in 872, under Bishop Wearfrith. The mill took fees, which were often paid in eels.

81. The Oxfam Shop (28 Wood Street)
The Tudor house is on the corner of Wood Street and Rother Street, and the first recorded occupier was Thomas Mitchell. He was the leaseholder, not the owner and he paid a rent of 20 shillings a year for the house and a plot of land. The shop was probably built in the 1540s, or it may have been extended or rebuilt in the 1590s, in the latter years of Queen Elizabeth I, the last Tudor monarch. It is said that the initials ER or IR, are visible on the lintel of the fireplace, which is hidden behind the main till of the shop. They could either be Elizabeth I

or James I, which poses a problem, when deciding when the house was really built.

What we see now, is a house, which includes 28 Wood Street, The Oxfam Shop and 27 and 26 Wood Street. The shop extends down the street, after a slight kink in the building for 16 feet. This kink in the building occurs on the first known plan in 1817 of the premises and so it is suggested that it has always been there. The house faces two ways. It faces a main thoroughfare, Wude Street (original spelling) and the Livestock Market – 'Rother Markite'. The plot of land on which the house was built, also contained two outhouses, which later became cottages, facing the Rother Market and separate from the house. The building, as it now stands and bearing in mind, the measurements, sits on a plot of land that was originally called a burgage plot. Stratford, when it was first planned, was divided up into burgage plots (200ft x 60ft), the frontage of the house jetties out onto the corner of Wood Street and Rother Street, supported by a dragon beam, and this presumably, was matched by a similar effect on the eastern side, where the cancer charity shop now stands. The timber supports are mounted by a carved face, which some have thought might be a zephyr. (The west wing is a 20th century edition). The house always contained one or more workshops and the four upper chambers were ideal as individual living areas for subletting.

The first tenant we know about is Richard Brinklow. He was an ironmonger who bought the lease in 1533 and paid an annual rent of 20 shillings and 8 pence for the whole leasehold. Until 1547, tenants of these premises, like Brinklow, paid rent to the Master of the Guild of the Holy Cross, representing the fraternity, whose chapel stands on the corner of Chapel Street and Church Street, i.e. the Guild Chapel. The church property was extensive and was laid out in burgage plots. The measure remains useful to understanding the footprints of many of the shops in Stratford.

In the year that King Henry VIII executed his fourth wife and was looking around for his fifth, he found time in his busy marital schedule, to order the suppression of the Guild. The rent, which formerly went to the Master of the Guild, was subsequently paid to the High Bailiff of a body which acted as trustees of the properties. The trustees are now the Town Trust, to whom Oxfam pays its rent.

William Parsons is probably the most well known tenant of the Tudor leasehold. William was an alderman, a one-time constable and twice High Bailiff of the Trustees of the former Guild Estates. It is from Parsons'

An historic photograph of Wood Street.

activities, that we learn most about the uses of the house and premises in the Tudor period.

Together with William Shakespeare, who was a close friend, he was charged with hoarding malt after bad harvests, while others were suffering. It is assumed that he used the premises and its barns and outbuildings for storage. Malt making was Stratford's major industry. His interest in the town led him to oppose the enclosures of the Welcombe Hills, which in turn, led Mr Rogers of Harvard House, coming round to his Wood Street home and attacking him.

Another High Bailiff assumed the lease. They were from one family, father and son, the Hiccox family. Father Hiccox leased the Maidenhead Inn which is now Shakespeare's Birthplace, as the family were wealthy landowners. It is believed that the Hiccox family may have used the building purely as a residence.

After the Hiccox era, it became a grocer chandler, whose owner's name was John Millward. Smallpox was in the town at this time and there were nine residents of the corner shop, four of which had smallpox. Many of these victims died and John Millward's daughter, Sarah, was one of them.

Two years before the accession of the young Queen Victoria in 1837, the Trustees of the Guild estates became an elected Town Council under new municipal laws. The oligarchies of families like the Hiccox family were finally replaced by elected representatives. It is thought, at about this time, the wooden Tudor house had the brickwork added.

Whatever the nature of this area, it always seems fairly crowded. From the census of 1861 we learn that there is a china shop at 26 Wood Street, at number 27 there is an agricultural labourer and in number 32, the smallest of the tenements, a wharf labourer. In all, 18 people were living in this L shaped property. A further claim to fame, suffragettes claimed equal rights through the windows of the upstairs bays.

82. The Manorial System

The manor was a key institution in the history of many villages and towns in England over several centuries. During the middle ages in particular, the manorial system affected everyone in society, from the highest lord to the humblest serf. Together with the church, it helped to determine how people lived their lives, influencing how they owned land, how they farmed, how they behaved to each other and how they interacted as part of the community.

Examples of the manors are found in Stratford. Alveston Manor, which is now a hotel, is situated, in what was, the manor of Stratford. Shottery Manor, which is now Stratford Grammar School for Girls, is situated in what was, Shottery manor. However, Stratford Manor has never had a manor house. Trade was the catalyst for the growth of Stratford.

The power of the manorial court dwindled and its hold on society was finally ended with the abolition of copyhold tenure in 1925. Manorial records are a valuable source for the medieval period, especially as they show the lives of ordinary men and women. Warwickshire is a county which has a strong tradition of manorial history, which is still being maintained today. Although few manorial courts are still allowed the right to meet. No less than three of them are to be found in Warwickshire. The courts of Alcester, Henley-in-Arden and Warwick continue to sit regularly to carry on their proud, local customs.

83. Inclosure Acts

(or Enclosure Acts in modern spelling)

(Wikipedia)

Where a series of UK acts of Parliament, which enclosed open fields and common land in the country, creating legal property rights to land that was previously considered common. Between 1604 and 1914, there were over 5,200 individual Inclosure Acts, inclosing 6.8 million acres of land. Prior to the inclosures in England, a portion of land was categorised as 'common' or 'waste'. Common land was under some kind of collective control. Called the open fields system, a single plot of land was divided among groups, often a lord employed participating peasants. This facilitated common grazing and crop rotation. Waste was the only land not officially claimed by any group, often cultivated by landless peasants.

Inclosures were also created so that landowners could charge higher rent to people working on the land. This was at least partially responsible for peasants leaving the countryside, to work in the city, in industrial factories.

84. The Borough of Stratford-upon-Avon Commons, Inclosures and Mills

Stratford was surrounded on all sides by common fields, which until the inclosures of 1775, abutted directly onto the north and west, and onto the outer limits of the town.

The only common for the Borough was the Bancroft and the rights of pasture there were, according to orders of the Court Leet in 1634, confined to freeholders who were limited to one horse or beast per person, sheep being prohibited altogether. The earliest reference to inclosures in Stratford occurs in Wolsey's inquisition of 1517-18, when Thomas Thomason was accused of having depopulated a messuage and 40 acres. The land between Shipston and Banbury Roads known as Bridgetown Field was inclosed in the last quarter of the 16th century.

On 28th October 1614, William Replingham of Great Harborough (agent for the principal landowner in Welcombe, William Combe), entered into an agreement with Shakespeare to recompense him and Thomas Greene for any damage they might suffer as lessees of the tithe. Whereas Shakespeare had assured Greene that the land would not be surveyed until the following April, the actual digging of the ditches was begun as soon as the frost had broken, on 19th December. The area of the land to be inclosed was seven or eight yardlands, or 400-600 acres, of which 200 acres was arable and the rest common greensward. It lay to the north of the town, probably between the present Clopton Road and the Golf Course, including the southern portion of what is now the park of Welcombe House and, on the north-east, a part of the Dingles.

The inclosure covered Stratford, Welcombe and Bishopton and allotments in lieu of land were made to 20 different persons. The land to be inclosed lay in the four fields known as the Rowley, Bishopton, Windmill Hill and Gild Pits Quarters and in the Common Meadows.

85. The Mop (Nicholas Fogg)
In 1196, Richard I granted the right to hold a market on Thursdays in Stratford-upon-Avon, in perpetuity.

Although the market day was changed to Fridays in the Victorian era, the weekly street market has been held ever since. For this privilege, Stratfordians paid their feudal lord, the Bishop of Worcester, 16 shillings annually. This charter was witnessed by an eminent company, which included the Archbishop of Canterbury, the Bishop of Normandy, and William of the Church of St Mary, perhaps the one in Warwick. It did not however, include the right to hold a fair. For this, the citizens had to wait until 1216, when a fair was granted on the eve, day and morrow of October 29th, the patronal festival of Holy Trinity Church. Other fairs were later granted on St Augustin's Day, Ascension Day and on 23rd December, one of the feasts of the Guild of the Holy Cross. This powerful religious community controlled medieval Stratford at the time.

Men hoping for employment, around 1900.

These fairs were not fairs in the sense we know them today. They were occasions when wares were sold and each fair specialised in a different commodity. One at least, was a horse fair. In a rare fit of flamboyance, Stratford Corporation bought a china faring for the curate's wife.

The first description of a fair in Stratford took place on the recreation ground during the jubilee in honour of Shakespeare, organised by the famous actor, David Garrick, in 1769. The fair was distinctive for many reasons. There was a side show with a Porcupine boy, a Man Tiger and a large collection of other kinds of birds, beasts and fishes, on the meadow, close to the theatre.

On 25th September each year, the ram and cheese fair was held. Rother Street would swarm with tumblers, fire eaters, poker swallowers and boxers. There was a considerable hop exchange and cheese was sold in such quantities that upwards of 200 wagon loads were brought in at one time.

The Mop, like the other fairs, dealt in a commodity but it was different from the others in that it was not food stuffs or livestock, but people. Men and women came to Stratford, in order to be hired by people looking for household servants.

The only one of these fairs to survive is the annual Mop, held in October, and being a Charter Mop, nobody but the reigning sovereign, can change it.

86. The Guildhall

Built in 1420, Stratford's Guildhall is where William Shakespeare attended school. According to Michael Wood, the famous historian, this is one of the most atmospheric, magical and important buildings in the whole of Britain.

In 2015, plans are to restore and open Stratford-upon-Avon's Guildhall, to make it possible for the public to see it for the first time. It is the room where Stratford-upon-Avon Town Council, for some decades, held their meetings.

87.   Shakespeare's Family Homes (Wikipedia)
Shakespeare's Birthplace in Henley Street is where the Bard was born and grew up. He was the son of John and Mary (née Arden) and one of eight children, five of which survived. His father used the house to make gloves. The name in those days was a whittawer. John Shakespeare was a dealer in hides and wool, and was elected to several municipal offices, serving as an alderman, a bailiff and the chief magistrate of the town, before he fell on hard times. His fortunes later revived after the success of his son and he was granted a coat of arms, five years before his death, probably paid for by his playwright son.

Mary Arden's Farm also known as Mary Arden's House, is the farmhouse owned by Mary Shakespeare, mother of William Shakespeare. It is located in the village of Wilmcote. It was bought by The Shakespeare Birthplace Trust in 1930 and furnished in the Tudor style. It is now the home of many rare breeds of animals.

Anne Hathaway's Cottage. Anne is believed to have grown up in Shottery. She assumed to have grown up at the Farmhouse which is the Hathaway family home. Her father, Richard Hathaway, was a yeoman farmer. He died in September 1581 and left Anne the sum of 6 pounds, 13 shillings and 4 pence, to be paid 'at the day of her marriage'. In her father's will, her name is listed as Agnes, leading to some scholars believing that she should be referred to as Agnes Hathaway, rather than Anne.

Anne Hathaway married William Shakespeare in November 1582, while pregnant with the couple's first child, to whom she gave birth six months later. Anne was nine years older than William, which some historians have given as evidence that it was a shotgun wedding. Another reason for her marrying later, is probably because she helped her mother look after her siblings.

Hall's Croft is the elegant Tudor home of Shakespeare's daughter Susannah and her husband Dr John Hall. The walled garden is planted with fragrant herbs, used in Dr Hall's remedies. Dr Hall married Susannah in 1607. The building now contains a collection of 16th and 17th century paintings and furniture. There is also an exhibition about Dr John Hall and the obscure medical practices of the period. Dr John Hall and Susannah, later moved to New Place, which William Shakespeare left to his daughter after his death.

New Place was William Shakespeare's final place of residence in Stratford. He died there in 1616. The house no longer exists and the land is owned by the Shakespeare Birthplace Trust.

In readiness for the anniversary of Shakespeare's death in 2016, the Shakespeare Birthplace Trust, with the aid of a large grant, is going to restore the garden. A reconstructed house is not to be built, but using architects and historians, the space where Shakespeare actually sat and wrote his plays, is to be constructed around a deep, awe inspiring pool. The position of the pool is the exact spot where Shakespeare wrote his last play, The Tempest. The house stood on the corner of Chapel Street and Chapel Lane and was apparently the second largest dwelling in the town. It was built in 1483 by Sir Hugh

Clopton, a wealthy London mercer and Lord Mayor. The house was built of timber and brick (then an innovation in Stratford). It had ten fireplaces, five handsome gables and grounds large enough to incorporate two barns and an orchard. It was built in 1843, three years after the Great Bridge over the River Avon, another gift from Sir Hugh Clopton.

88. Robert Mansell Smith

Councillor Mansell Smith lived in Mansell Street. He was mayor in 1930-31 and President of the Royal British Legion 1944-49.

Councillor Mansell Smith was responsible for amalgamating his many charities to form the four alms house charities and three grant giving charities, seven in all. His father, John Mansell Smith, was mayor before him, in 1921-22.

89. The Firsts

The first recorded bailiff was Thomas Gilbert 1553-54. There is a stained glass window in the Guild Chapel in his memory.

The first town clerk was in 1554-68 – Richard Simons.

The first high steward was in 1610 – George Baron Carew of Clopton.

The first mayor was in 1661-62 – Robert Butler.

The author has also discovered that in 1752-53, Harry Preston, mayor, abdicated.

90. The Mayor's Parlour

The Mayor's Parlour is the first door on the left, as you enter Stratford Town Hall. It is there for the use of the

Councillor Cyril Kemp and his wife Carol.

Mayor during his year in office. The above picture shows Councillor Cyril Kemp and his wife Carol, during their term of office (1963-1964). In the picture, it shows the panelling on the walls to be painted white. Visitors nowadays, will see them restored to their original state.

91. The Flower Family

The Flower family are well known in Stratford. Edward Flower, son of Richard Fordham Flower, was born in 1862 and four times Mayor. His son, Charles Edward Flower was born in 1879 and had two brothers, Edgar and William. Archibald Flower was born in 1915 and his son was Fordham Flower, who had a daughter, Elizabeth Flower, the current generation.

92. King Richard III

He was born on 2 October 1452 and died at the Battle of Bosworth on 22 August 1485. King Richard III's body was found under a car park in Leicester in 2012, but a group calling themselves the Plantagenet Alliance, insisted that he had wanted to be buried in York Minster. Two justices ruled there were no public law grounds for interfering with the plans to rebury the King in Leicester.

Richard was killed in battle and was England's last medieval king. The King's funeral will be televised in the spring of 2015.

93.   The Magna Carta (Wikipedia)

In June 2015, it will be 800 years since the Magna Carta was sealed between the barons of medieval England and King John. Magna Carta is Latin and means Great Charter. The Magna Carta was one of the most important documents of medieval England. It was sealed between the feudal barons and King John at Runnymede, near Windsor Castle. The document was a series of written promises between the King and his subjects, that he, the King, would govern England and deal with its people, according to the customs of feudal law. 2015 is the 800th anniversary of its sealing and the four known parchments of the Magna Carta have been brought together for 2015 only, and are displayed in the British Library.

The Magna Carta was an attempt by the barons, to stop a king, in this case, John, abusing his power, with the people of England suffering.

England had, for some years, owned land in France. The barons had provided the King with both money and men to defend this territory. Traditionally, the King had always consulted the barons, before raising taxes (as they had to collect it) and demanding more men for military service (as they had to provide the men). This was all part of the feudal system.

Following his constant demands for money and men, and by 1204, losing his land in northern France, John introduced high taxes without asking the barons. The Magna Carta was written by the barons to prevent this happening.

94. The Fluffing

Many residents of Stratford-upon-Avon travel daily to London and have to use the underground system to reach their destinations. Unknown to many commuters, when the current is turned off late at night, gangs of men and women, walk the tunnels, clearing the floor of hair and fibres from clothing. This, when collected, is a huge amount of material. Without these men and women, the underground system would not be able to operate.

95. Hats

Hats began to be worn in the late 16th century. The term, milliner, comes from the Italian city of Milan, where the best quality hats were made in the 18th century.

As with all things, if not careful, traditions tend to get lost. Men, when wearing a hat, should remove it on the threshold. Alternatively, women keep their hats on and in days gone by, were never allowed to remove them, except when sitting down for luncheon or dinner, but they remained on for tea.

A male mayor wears a bicorn hat and a female mayor wears a tricorn. Hopefully, this tradition will continue in Stratford-upon-Avon for years to come.

Corinthians, Ch11, V2: Remember me in everything and maintain traditions, even as I deliver them to you. (The author puts this in as a reference from the bible to traditions).

96. Stratford Stations

As stated earlier, (Index No.4), the steel road arrived in Stratford-upon-Avon in 1859, which opened Stratford-upon-Avon to tourists. In1873, Stratford Station was one of two, the original being in its present position on Alcester Road in 1859. Old Town was built in 1909, where Mrs May Jordan was the manageress of Stratford Old Town Refreshment Room at Stratford Old Town Station, from 1915 to 1934. Remnants of the platform on Severn Meadows Road, can still be seen.

The third station, Stratford Parkway, at Bishopton, was opened on 20th May 2013. The station cost 6.9 million pounds and the first passenger train stopped on Sunday 2nd June 2013. It is named as the Warwickshire Sustainable Transport Project, funded by the Department of Transport. It is operated by London Midland under a three year agreement.

97. Welcombe House

The Welcombe House is now the Welcombe Hotel and Welcombe House was part of the Manor of Old Stratford. It was granted in 1537 to John Combe, then in 1663, to William Combe. In 1835, it was bought by Mark Phillips, a cotton manufacturer from Manchester and one of Manchester's first members of parliament. It was built in the neo-Jacobean style. The Phillips family gifted it to the Trevelyan family.

98. Reorganisation of Local Government
(See also Index No. 20)

On 1st April 2015, the wards of Stratford District are to be changed yet again, following the direction of the Boundary Commission of Great Britain. Stratford's ward boundaries have been changed to make the nine wards that make up the parish of Stratford-upon-Avon, as equal as possible, per capita.

From 1 April 2015, the names are to be: Avenue, Clopton, Welcombe, Tiddington, Bridgetown, Guild Hall, Shottery, Hathaway and Bishopton. The new parish boundary is incorporating the old parish of Stratford and Old Drayton. Each of the wards of Stratford parish are to be represented by one district councillor and two town councillors. The county council representatives are not up for election in 2015. The number of district councillors sitting on Stratford District Council are to be considerably reduced. The number of councillors sitting on Stratford Town Council are to remain the same. Coincidentally, there is also to be a General Election in 2015.

99.   Alveston Old Church

(Brian Johnson and Anne Warenhauser)

At the end of Mill Lane in Alveston, next to the half-timbered old vicarage, stands the old church of St James with its small churchyard. The church is in a dominant position on a mound, suggesting the foundations of an earlier building. It is well placed on the edge of the meadows that lead down to the River Avon, at a height which the river almost, but never quite reaches. Across the river, the steep profile of Hatton Rock dominates the scene. Between the church and the river, signs of medieval strip farming can clearly be seen, particularly in the evening when the sun is low in the sky. The churchyard is small in relation to the size of the church. The grave stones are tilting or have fallen and their lettering lost.

The history of the area is not fully clear but it has been settled since the Iron Age (800BC-42AD). The area was attractive for a settlement because it enjoyed rich soil that sat on top of sand and gravel terraces. The terrain was created by a series of glaciers that gouged out the Avon valley and laid down rich alluvial silt. The valley is clearly delineated by the sandstone of Hatton Rock and the limestone of the Cotswolds. The crops flourished and the river provided a constant supply of fresh water. There are a number of Iron Age sites along the Avon; Longbridge, Wasperton, Alveston and Bidford.

Alveston parish is well positioned on the river and a nearby supply of salt. Salt was important, not for seasoning food but for preserving it, to be eaten over the winter months when fresh meat was unavailable. At Droitwich, some 25 miles away, there was an abundance of salt. A network of salt ways became established, in order to transport salt around the country. One of these ran from Droitwich to Stratford and then onwards to Banbury. In prehistoric times, there were no roads suitable for wheeled vehicles, so packhorses and mules were used. These had to follow tracks with a firm footing so ridges were popular, but they also had to have access to water. It is possible that Alveston parish benefited from this passing trade, which came across the river where Clopton Bridge is allocated today. It then went up Loxley Road towards Croft School. It later met up with the current Banbury Road near Goldicote.

In Anglo Saxon times, from 410AD, Warwickshire was settled by two German tribes; Anglians travelling from the east and settling in the Upper Avon valley and then the Thame Blythe basin, and the West Saxons moving northwards from the Thames and Severn valleys into the middle Avon area, and south Warwickshire.

They were pagan and the earliest groups cremated their dead. Later, burial replaced cremation and people were buried with their personal ornaments and weapons. Important burial sites include one in Alveston behind the Alveston Manor Hotel.

When the Romans conquered Britain in 43AD, they improved upon the earlier routes and more trading took place. Alveston probably enjoyed increased trade, though no details are available. The Romans set up a camp, just outside the parish, on Orchard Hill, along the Shipston Road opposite the turning to Clifford Chambers. Their camp between Tiddington and Stratford, was non-military. It was situated on what at the moment, is an open field, between the settlements of Tiddington and Stratford. Excavations have shown several roads leaving this site, including routes towards Wellesbourne and Alderminster.

100. Population
The Domesday Survey of 1086, revealed that the whole of England had only 1.5 million people living in it. The parish of Alveston, including Tiddington, had 43 families plus one female slave, about 216 people in all. Stratford-upon-Avon had only 28 families, with a total population of 200.

101. Vicarages
Alveston parish has had four vicarages. A building was required to house the priest, who officiated in the church. At present, archaeological evidence of an earlier building than that which remains and now called the

Old Vicarage, has not been found. However, there are references to it in the records. In December 1374, the vicar at the time, had let his house fall into decay, and it was described as being in a ruinous state.

The first vicarage accompanying the old church, situated next door, is dated from the early 16th century and is Grade II listed.

In a church terrier (a book describing the site, the boundaries, the acreage, the tenants etc. of certain lands), compiled for the Bishop in 1585, he states that his house consists of three bays. There is also a three bayed barn with a little house of one bay adjoining it. Houses usually consisted of timber with wattle and daub infill. The number of main supports or trusses between each infill, gives the size of the house. This space is called a bay and ranges from two and half to six metres. Generally the majority of houses were two to four bays in length. As building technology improved, separate barns were built for the use of livestock and chimneys were added to existing houses, enabling the high spaces in the open hall to be used.

* * * *

The past is past and will never return
Our future is not known
Only the present is truly our own

(Sue Thompson)

- VOLUME 4 -

102. Agincourt (Stratford Herald)

600 years ago on 25th October 1415, King Henry V led his army into battle at Agincourt. The battle was fought and won on the fields of France, yet the road to Agincourt is said to have begun with a very surprising event here in Warwickshire. King Henry V visited Kenilworth Castle on the eve of the anniversary which fell on 24th October, which was his favoured residence. It was whilst staying there in 1414/15 that he reportedly received from the French, an insulting gift of pilas (tennis balls).

The incident was recorded by chronicler and monk, John Streeche, who writing shortly after the King's death, wrote that the French embassy to the King "foolishly said that they would send to Henry King of England, because he was young, little balls to play with and soft pillows to sleep on to help him grow to manly strength".

The meaning was clear – the French implied that the King, who was not yet 30 years old, was too childish to engage in the serious kingly practice of diplomacy and warfare.

It is debatable whether Henry's gift from the French was indeed the spur to his invasion of Normandy, but it was recorded as such later. This incident features in Shakespeare's play, King Henry V and it was certainly the gift of tennis balls that gave Henry his decisive impetus to war.

King Henry V, the play, was performed in the 600th anniversary year of the Battle of Agincourt, on the

Stratford stage, with Alex Hassell playing the part of the King. Jayne Lapotaire was also in the cast, she lives nearby.

103. The Unicorn Public House

The Unicorn Public House sat on Bridgefoot, where the Pen & Parchment now sits. Its gardens stretched right down towards the Warwick Road and this was known as Unicorn Meadow. It is famous because the gardens were often flooded during the winter months and doubled up as the town skating rink. The multi-storey car park sits on its footprint. The extension of the car park for some years and until recently, was called Unicorn Meadow but sadly things move on and the name has disappeared. It was built in the late 18th century and is a Grade II listed building, being listed on 9th February 1972. The interior has many exposed beams, some probably reused, one overlay moulded and one richly moulded. The large barn, not included, is said to have been used as a theatre in the late 18th or 19th century but has been much altered.

104. The Bus Station

Stratford has had a bus station for many, many years. It was still in operation when the author came to Stratford in 1978. It was owned by the Midland Red Bus Company. The buses entered from and exited onto the Warwick Road. Because of its single ownership, it was sold for housing and a three storey block of flats now stands on its footprint. The residents of Stratford would love to see the return of a bus station, but where to put it, proves to be the problem, as there is not sufficient land owned by the bus companies to open a multi company bus station.

105. The Dirty Duck (The Shakespeare Blog)

Otherwise known as The Black Swan or vice versa. In 1556, John Shakespeare's first appointment in Stratford-upon-Avon was as ale taster, requiring him to check the measures, prices and quality of the beer provided by innkeepers. As a market town, Stratford always provided refreshment to visitors, locals and traders. By the mid 19th century, the local Flower's brewery was making some of the best beer to be found in England. In 1851 the Board of Health listed all licensed houses of which there were 85 in Stratford. Many have been demolished, changed use or have different names. Quite a few owed their names to the Shakespeare connection.

There was once a Globe Inn in Great William Street and a Falstaff Inn at the top of Henley Street. Others, like The Falcon, The Garrick and The Shakespeare Hotel itself, have kept their names and are still trading. Sadly, bearing in mind the number of scenes set in the London tavern, there has never been a Boar's Head in Stratford, to my knowledge. Part of Shakespeare's birthplace itself, became a pub after Shakespeare's time, the famous Swan and Maidenhead. In W S Brassington's book, 'Shakespeare's Homeland', it states that the Dirty Duck bears the reputation of having sheltered Shakespeare, when he fled across the river from St Thomas Lucy's men (an event which probably never took place).

The Dun Cow Inn on the Birmingham Road (no longer in existence) was the reputed rendezvous of the poet and his companions after their poaching expeditions. It is said that the venison was cooked before the "ample fireplace" of that inn.

The Black Swan/Dirty Duck has a strong connection with Shakespeare that continues to this day and that makes it famous among visitors. The central part of the building has been a public house since 1738, known as the Black Swan since at least 1776. The bar to the right of the entrance was originally a separate house, incorporated into the pub in 1866, because of the growing use of the river for pleasure. The building to the left became part of the pub in 1937.

The theatre's connection with the pub, goes back over 100 years. One of the actors from Frank Benson's theatre company, (visiting Stratford from 1910 to 1915) made a collection of plays, poems and letters which are now in the Shakespeare Centre Library and Archive.

Stratford pubs nowadays, including this one, are more respectable. But the sign hanging outside shows both faces of the public house, the dignified Black Swan on one side and the mischievous, boozy Dirty Duck on the other side, facing the theatres. It is thought that it was the actors who gave the pub its nickname, by which it is universally known.

106. Escape Arts (The Slaughterhouse Project)

(Stratford-upon-Avon Focus Magazine)

In 2014, Stratford Town Trust (formed in 2002) promoted a competition called the Million Pound Project, to bring forward some exciting new ventures in old buildings in Stratford. One of the winners, was Escape Arts and it was an ambitious heritage project, in the autumn of 2014. The old slaughterhouse, situated between Sheep Street and Bridge Street was to be the new venue. The building began to reveal its secrets from the past. In the back room of the slaughterhouse, a second lower floor leading to a possible cellar and then hidden windows were found behind the roof lights.

Initial investigations at Birthplace Archive offered the answers to the building's past. From records, the sale of the business was made by Nathanial Cooper, a rope maker, for whom a long premises would be ideal, to John Gill, a wine merchant in 1832. (The cellar may have been used for storing wine). By February 1880 there was an auction of 14 Bridge Street by butcher, Joseph Farmer, with a rent set at 7 pounds, 10 shillings and a couple of capons.

In the 1891 Census, No 13 Bridge Street was occupied by 32 year old harness maker, William White, who would have made full use of the stables adjoining the slaughterhouse. The renovation of the slaughterhouse in 1895 revealed more details of the cellar that went down to a depth of seven feet, and were amazingly detailed in quote documents provided by builders John Harris.

By 1896, 13/14 Bridge Street saw the start of the Henson era, which continued into the 1960s in the shape of Brian Henson, who has been able to pass on stories and information about his family business that was so integral to the town.

In 1986 Brian's grandfather James, went first into business with the local Jordan family. A long term lease was set with the added stipulation for a couple of good capons. By 1898, Hensons the butchers were well established and took on their first apprentice.

Life for apprentices was tough in the Victorian era. The signed apprentice document stipulates that Harold James Mullis, "shall not haunt taverns or playhouses, play cards or dice, nor absent himself from his said master's service, day or night, unlawfully." He was not allowed to get married or waste the goods of the master. In 1900 James Henson took on his second apprentice,

Percy Albert Betteridge, from Wellesbourne. The first World War interrupted Mr Henson's plans.

The role of Brian Henson's father, Stanley, who later took over the family business in the First World War, is detailed in Harry Drinkwater's award winning diaries. His experiences include the Warwickshire Regiment on the Western Front. References made to the injuries that Stanley suffered, when, amongst others, he was hit by a shell in a trench at three o'clock one morning. These injuries did not prevent Stanley from taking over the business in 1918.

In 1932, the slaughterhouse underwent another refurbishment with £5,000 being spent under the terms of the new lease. Hensons were now renowned for their pork pies with regular advertisements in the Herald.

Stanley retired in 1965 when Hensons became Baxters. Baxters continued to operate in the building for nine years. Livestock continued to be purchased at Stratford Market and from local farmers, and were slaughtered in the slaughterhouse.

Stanley Henson, 4ᵗʰ from right, smoking a pipe/cigar.

The slaughterhouse was left virtually untouched until the summer of 2014, with the arrival of Escape Arts. Escape Arts became a charity in 2007, Escape Arts itself having been founded by Robin Wade in 1997 and Community Art in Action was founded by Karen Williams. In 1997, these two organisations joined forces under a shared vision. The ethos of Escape Arts is involvement, encouraging and empowering people to reach their potential.

The slaughterhouse project has been delivered through the vision of the project manager, Karen Williams, and has been set up to tell the history of Stratford and its people, through art.

107. Stratford-upon-Avon Butterfly Farm
(Wikipedia)

The Butterfly Farm was opened by David Bellamy in 1985. Richard Lamb, the manager, has been managing this farm since its inception.

Stratford Butterfly Farm is one of Stratford's very popular visitor attractions. A leafy, tropical environment is simulated inside large greenhouses. There are numerous free flying butterflies, some five inches across and a few free flying birds and a pool containing fish with running water. There are also insects and spiders living in glass displays (thank goodness!).

It consists of three main areas, a caterpillar room, which houses caterpillars, pupae, eggs and specialist plants for butterfly breeding. The farm is renowned for sending many of their species far and wide, to other breeders in the UK and around the world.

The Insect City houses more exotic insects, such as beetles, Praying Mantises, stick insects and giant millipedes. A section in Insect City is called Mini Beast and has snails and crabs.

Arachnoland houses over 15 species of spider, from Black Widows to tarantulas. They also house the world's largest spider, the Goliath Bird Eater. This section also includes a selection of Imperial Scorpions that glow in the dark.

108. The Gunpowder Plot (Wikipedia)

The plan of the Gunpowder Plot was to blow up the House of Lords during the state opening of England's Parliament, on 5th November 1605. Robert Catesby embarked on the scheme after hopes of securing greater religious tolerance under King James I of England and VI of Scotland, had faded, leaving many English Catholics disappointed. His fellow plotters were John Wright, Thomas Wintour, Thomas Percy, Guy Fawkes, Robert Keys, Thomas Bates, Robert Wintour, Christopher Wright, John Grant, Ambrose Rookwood, Sir Everard Digby and Francis Tresham. Fawkes himself, had ten years of military experience fighting in the Spanish Netherlands, in suppression of the Dutch Revolt and was given charge of the explosives. The plot was revealed to the authorities in an anonymous letter, which had been sent to William Parker, Fourth Baron Monteagle, on 26th October 1605. During a search of the House of Lords, at about midnight, on 4th November 1605, Fawkes was discovered guarding 36 barrels of gunpowder, enough to reduce the House of Lords to rubble, and was arrested. Most of the conspirators fled from London, as they learnt of the plot's discovery, trying to enlist support along the way.

The conspirators started their plotting in many large

houses in and around Stratford town. One house in particular, Coughton Court, near Alcester, witnessed some of the most defining moments in British History, when some of the conspirators were plotting within it.

(A word about the author. Joan's husband, Ian, is allegedly related to Guy Fawkes, through his mother, Helen Fawkes.)

109. Murder and Crime

(Murder & Crime Series, Nick Billingham)

The town of Stratford is most famous for Shakespeare and the fact that it is a small, market town, but beneath the surface of all towns and villages lurk some disturbing stories. The first mention, is Charlotte Clopton, who was entombed in Holy Trinity Church and when the vault was opened for another burial, she was found to be standing, having awoken in her coffin, but unable to get out. This is reputedly to have inspired the tomb scene from Romeo and Juliet. Another Clopton legend states that Margaret Clopton, having been dumped by her young man, lost the plot and threw herself down a well. She was destined to become the role model for Ophelia in Hamlet. Stratford is peculiarly marked with some odd and unsolved cases.

The Meon Hill murder remains an almost archetypal case and the real facts now lie almost buried amidst a welter of superstition and misinformation. This famous murder has got all the elements of a mystery and remains unsolved to this day. Meon Hill is a pretty odd place. It is one of the outliers of the Cotswold Hills and it looms on the horizons of the Avon Valley. On its summit are the remains of an iron age fort, ditches and mounds, left over from an era, long before modern man. The hill has always been treated with a kind of reverence. Perhaps the mystic element was assured from the very start of the investigation.

The date of the murder could also be significant. 14th February has long been associated with pagan fertility rights. On 14th February 1945, Charles Walton, went off to work on laying a hedge on the side of Meon Hill and this was the last time anyone saw him definitely alive. By all accounts, he was a pretty cantankerous old man. He was 74 and had bad arthritis, which probably accounts for his cantankerousness. He had always been a farm labourer in the district and was working part time for Mr Potter of Firs Farm, doing odd jobs to stretch out his pension. He lived with his niece, Edith, in the village and there was nothing particularly dramatic to note that he wasn't well liked. This day passed like any other and it wasn't until he failed to return home in the afternoon, that anyone really gave a thought to him. Three of his friends walked up to the hedge where he had been working. Luckily, Alfred Potter and Harry Beasley were slightly ahead of Edith, when they found Charles' body. They managed to stop her seeing the full horror.

Charles Walton lay on the ground by the hedge with a pitchfork stuck in his neck and massive wounds to his chest. The billhook was still sticking out of his ribs. His braces had been broken in the struggle and his pockets were turned inside out. He had been struck three times with the billhook and then pierced with the pitchfork. Whoever attacked him had made quite sure that he would never get up again. Fabian of Scotland Yard, came up from London by the night train. Fabian also ordered aerial photographs to be taken by the RAF but it all revealed a complete absence of clues. Fabian obviously hadn't reached any conclusion and returned to London, where he started to write his memoirs.

Murder of William Hiron (Nick Billingham)

Throughout the summer of 1820, the roads around Stratford were getting more and more dangerous to travel. It was getting to the stage when travelling alone was courting disaster if you were rich. The recession was due to the fact soldiers were coming back from the war in France, only to find that many of their rights had been removed. It was only a matter of time before tragedy struck.

At dawn on Sunday 5th November 1820, William Hiron was discovered lying in a ditch with massive head injuries. John Ashfield, the Stratford Constable, was called out to the scene of the crime and soon discovered that the assault had taken place at Littleham Bridge on the Wellesbourne Road, a mile from where William was found. There was a pool of blood in the middle of the road and signs of a brutal struggle. William's horse had found its own way back to Alveston during the night. John Ashfield found no clues as to the gang who were at the scene, but he had his suspicions. William Hiron rallied a little once they got him home, enough to say, "three villains". But then he lapsed into a coma.

One prime suspect was a petty criminal by the name of Thomas Heytreay. The rumours were that he had some blood on him. His sister had been hanged at Warwick that April, after being found guilty of cutting the throat of her mistress at Dial House Farm. Ann Heytreay insisted she had no idea what strange mood came over her and made her commit such a grisly murder, but that was not enough to stop them hanging her. Thomas must have been tainted with the same criminal trait.

William Hiron died of his injuries on the Tuesday and the executors of his Will, posted a reward of 200 guineas for the conviction of his murderers. John Ashfield tracked down Thomas Heytreay at Mr Bradley's farm on Thursday morning and immediately charged him with the murder. The matter was deeply serious for Thomas, because if he was found guilty of the crime, he would certainly go to the gallows. In the farm parlour, Mr Greenway laid out the whole reward money in cash and suggested that if Thomas revealed who else was in the plot, he may well get the money and a free pardon. He promptly confessed that it was all the idea of Samuel Sidney, Henry Adams and Nathanial Quinney. He also suggested he was the victim and had taken no part in the actual attack, trying to weasel his way out of trouble.

Once all four highway robbers were in custody, it fell to Mr Ashfield to try and find some evidence to confirm Thomas Heytreay's confession. The town's lock up was far too small to properly question all four suspects. Since John Ashfield lived at The Falcon Inn, it was decided to question them there. The four were given as much ale as they could drink, which seems to have been plenty. They were then individually interrogated, again with the reward money and a possible promise of being pardoned, held out as an incentive. It wasn't long before all four confessed. The reward money was then withdrawn and no one could remember saying anything about the free pardon. The four were promptly sent to Warwick to be tried for murder and were hanged at Warwick Gaol two days later.

The ambush at Littleham Bridge, although the plot was originally to waylay the bailiff from a nearby farm, who would have been returning from market with lots of cash. The fog was so thick, it was thought that it was a case of mistaken identity.

110. Waterside

(A History of Streets and Buildings, Robert Bearman)

The biggest change in Waterside during the 19th century, was the refronting of numerous little cottages in brick. Several new ones were also built, Nos 36 to 37 for example, in 1829. Nos 32 to 33, and 34 to 35, also in the 1820s. A very handsome row, Nos 40 to 43, was built in 1856/57, but it was not until 1887, when the Lecture Hall, now the Theatre workshops, was built, that any striking addition to the street's appearance, was made. The architect, Arthur Flower, chose to build in imitation Tudor, as he later did for the technical school in Henley Street.

The 20th century brought further changes, the most attractive being No 45, now part of the Thistle Hotel, built in 1915, to the designs of Albert H Calloway, for Miss Annie Justins, the proprietor of the Shakespeare Hotel and later, Stratford's first lady Mayor (Joan was number six).

Waterside has lived with the threat of flooding for many years. A plaque on the wall of No 18, recalls the deluge of 1st January 1901, as the worst in recent times, apparently, breaking a record set in a flood of 1801, the last one being 10th December 2013. However, there were several before that.

The horse drawn line functioned for several decades, but did not prosper. In 1851 the Oxford, Worcester and

Wolverhampton Railway was opened through Moreton in Marsh and the tramway began experimenting with steam operation.

In 1859, the southern section between Moreton and Shipston was converted into a proper railway. The tramway company went bankrupt in 1868 and the line was taken over by the Great Western Railway.

111. The Tercentenary (Marian Pringle)
Before the tercentenary of Shakespeare's birth was celebrated in 1864, plans were discussed in Stratford and London, to decide how a suitable memorial to William Shakespeare should be created. Three ideas were put forward. First, for a school of drama to be endowed in London, second for the embellishment of the Shakespeare family properties and third, for a statue. Edward Flower, Stratford brewer, was a leader in the plans to celebrate the tercentenary, the family being a major financial supporter. But eventually, it took place in the form of a great timber pavilion, put up on part of the land in Southern Lane that Charles Flower, Edward's son, would later purchase when he built his family home, Avon Bank. The tercentenary fortnight included a ball, Handel's Messiah and several Shakespearian performances, which turned out to be a financial disaster. The pavilion was dismantled and sold off. Bancroft itself is interesting, being a large expanse of low lying land adjacent to the river – literally the bank field. This was earmarked as common land and is where the burgesses could turn out their cattle, horses, sheep and pigs. As the population grew, rules had to be imposed to limit the numbers and during the Elizabethan period, sheep were restricted to an hour's

grazing. Pigs had to be kept on a lead. It is alleged that soon afterwards, the rates changed and became so high that only the better off could afford them. Subsequently, the land degenerated into waste.

112. The Stratford Canal

(Continued from Cameo 67 in Volume 3)

The event which transformed the Bancroft, was the arrival of the canal in 1816. It began in 1793 at Kings Norton and took 20 years to complete. The line to the Bancroft was not finalised until 1814 and was opened two years later into the canal basin which still survives. In 1823, the Earl of Plymouth, to whom any wasteland in the town, belonged, sold the site of this basin to the Canal Company and in 1827, the rest of the Bancroft for the construction of a second basin. The arm which connected the two, can still be seen. Although in 1901, this latter was filled in. The reason for this expansion was the completion of a terminus on the Bancroft, and the Stratford to Moreton in Marsh horse drawn tramway opened in 1826. This pioneer venture is commemorated only by the attractive brick footbridge, affectionately known as the Tramway Bridge.

While the canal and the tramway flourished, this remained a busy area with both basins lined with wharfs and warehouses, all linked by a network of lines. Coal was the principal commodity, with no less than 14 coal wharfs on the Bancroft area by 1815, with two timber wharfs, a stone wharf and a lead and glass wharf. There were two dry docks managed by a boat builder, Thomas Kent, and a timber merchant's business, established by James Cox in 1893. It was subsequently moved to its current position, i.e. Cox's Yard.

The whole area was thus transformed in little more than a decade, from a piece of scrubland, to a bustling commercial centre. For a time, trade flourished, but neither the canal nor the tramway could cope with the competition from the railways, which reached Stratford in 1859/60. Trade fell away and by the 1870s, the time was approaching, for a second transformation of the Bancroft, this time into a recreational area.

(For further information on the canal see Cameo 131)

113. History of Theatre Peformance in Stratford

It is well known that the first performance of a Shakespeare play took place in the Town Hall on 9th September 1746. The process started with Charles Flower's acquisition of the Bancroft, for the building of a Shakespeare Memorial Theatre. This, built to the designs of Edward Dodgshun and William Unsworth, opened in 1879, although the buildings were not completed until 1881. The style was startling, nothing remotely like it, had ever been seen in the town, a collection of pointed towers and spires, in an ornate mixture of brick, stone and timber. Much of this extraordinary building was burnt down in 1826, although the Picture Gallery, fronting Waterside, survived together with its fine terracotta panels, by Paul Kummer and also the walls of the semi-circular auditorium, which had projected to the south.

The new theatre designed by Elizabeth Scott, opened in 1932. It was considered an intrusion into the town's ancient traditions. The new theatre incorporated what had survived of the older building and then in the mid-1980s, the conference hall was converted into another auditorium, The Swan. The main alteration was to instate a roof, similar to the one that had graced the original 1879 building. The theatre was set in osier beds to the south and this is where Lord Ronald Gower's fine statue of Shakespeare was put in 1888 and was subsequently moved to its present position (more detail can be found in Volume 1).

The second basin, closer to Clopton Bridge, was filled in, despite objections from Marie Corelli in 1901 and became a public park, complete with bandstand, in 1913. The town end of the Bancroft, which had been acquired by Charles Flower, became a public park, complete with bandstand. The original canal basin survived but grew increasingly stagnant and when the new theatre was opened, the site was cleared and the Gower memorial moved from its original position, to where it is now.

It is alleged that the Pen & Parchment Public House at Bridgefoot was also used for performing Shakespeare's plays.

114. The Tramway

The Stratford to Moreton tramway, was a 16 mile long, horse drawn wagon way, from the Canal Basin in Stratford, to Moreton in Marsh, with a branch to Shipston on Stour. An Act of Parliament was passed in 1821 and construction completed in 1826. The branch line to Shipston on Stour was completed in 1836.

The Tramway was intended to carry Black Country coal to the rural districts of southern Warwickshire via the canal and limestone and agricultural produce northwards. The route was surveyed by the railway promoter William James and engineered by John Urpeth Rastrick.

115. The Memorial Theatre Fire 1926

When the Edward Flower Memorial Theatre burnt down, William Bridges Adams, who was the artistic director at the time, moved all the productions to the cinema in Greenhill Street. On her first visit to Stratford, as a holiday maker, Joan saw Gone with the Wind in this cinema.

Elizabeth Scott's new theatre was opened by the Prince of Wales, Edward VIII, in 1932.

116. The Mayor's Chain

The chains and jewels worn by mayors are of comparatively recent origin. Up until the end of the 18th century, only 11 towns possessed them. Unlike swords, caps of maintenance, maces etc., they have no special significance, apart from making out the wearer as a person of importance. The life of a chain began in the theatre, because most of the groundlings in Shakespeare's time, could neither read nor write. To make the play easier to understand, chains were worn by the principal characters.

The gold chain or collar of the Mayor of Stratford-upon-Avon, comprises 13 links of "SS" in shape, alternating with 12 shields of arms. In the front, is an oval medallion portrait of Shakespeare in enamel.

117. Lady Mayors (Since 1928)

In 1928, when women were given the vote, it was possible for the first time to have a Lady Mayor in Stratford:

1928-29 Annie Justins
1953-54 Muriel Phillips

1956-57 Eleanor Waldron
1970-71 Muriel Pogmore
1976-77 Sarah Wheeler
1995-96 Joan McFarlane
1998-99 Maureen Beckett
1999-2000 Angela Colbeck
2000-01 Juliet Short
2002-03 Sheila Price
2008-09 Donna Barker
2009-10 Joyce Taylor
2010-11 Jenny Fradgley
2011-12 Shelagh Sandle
2015-16 Diane Walden
2016-17 Tessa Bates

118. First Women Graduates
Admitted to Cambridge University

The author's mother was one of these, born in 1889, Nora Pickering, attended lectures, took examinations and gained honours in those examinations. They were however, unable to receive the degree, to which, had they been men, their examinations would have entitled them. The new university statute of 1920 which admitted women to full membership of the University, and which came into effect from October that year, enabled women who had previously taken and gained honours, in university examinations, to return to matriculate and to have the degree to which they were entitled, conferred on them. Consequently, at the very first ceremony at which women were able to graduate, more than 40 women did so. Nora Pickering was one of these. She gained a first class honours in Latin and Greek and a first class honours degree in modern languages. She married

Charles Crosbee in 1928, he having been in his father's jewellery business, a pilot in the Royal Flying Corps and returned to run the jewellery business subsequently. During the Second World War, the jewellery business was taken over by the Ministry of Defence, to make aircraft engine parts.

119. King Henry VIII

He was the third child and second son of Henry VII. He was born on 28 June 1491 and died on 28 January 1547 and is buried in St George's Chapel, Windsor. On 12 October 1537, Jane Seymour, bore him his only legitimate son, Prince Edward, the future Edward VI and sadly she died soon after from an infection. Edward VI came to the throne at the age of 10. He was a sickly child and the country was run by his protectors, firstly, the Duke of Somerset, his mother's brother, then by the Duke of Northumberland. Edward died at the age of 16 in 1553.

'King Henry VIII' was co-authored by William Shakespeare and John Fletcher and was written in 1613. It was recorded at the time under its alternative title, All is True. The Royal Shakespeare Company performed the play in 2006, as part of their Complete Works festival. Donald Sinden, later to become Sir Donald Sinden, played King Henry VIII in 1970. He lived, when in Stratford, in Tiddington and drove a black taxi to avoid recognition. Joan ran across Donald Sinden cutting the hedge, adjacent to the Tramway Bridge, on one of her walks into Stratford. When asked why, Sir Donald replied, "somebody has to do it".

Sir Donald Sinden CBE FRSA 9th October 1923 – 12th September 2014

120. Ditty Number One

As taught to Joan by her father in childhood

> *On Monday I pulled out the motor*
>
> *On Tuesday I gave it a clean*
>
> *On Wednesday and Thursday, a crowd gathered round and said, 'what a lovely machine!'*
>
> *On Friday I filled it with petrol and rubbed it all over with lard*
>
> *On Saturday morning it started to rain so I shoved it back into the yard*

121. The Shakespeare Birthplace Trust
(Henley Street)

This building was the site of the White Lion public house. The cellars of Shakespeare's Birthplace Trust are renowned because they store priceless artefacts, dating back centuries, being air conditioned and secure. These were the wine cellars of the pub.

122. Bridges (Wikipedia)

There are two foot bridges that cross the River Avon as well as the five other bridges mentioned elsewhere. The Lucy's Mill Bridge has been referred to before but The Tramway Bridge not so frequently.

The Stratford and Moreton Tramway was a 16 mile (25km) horse drawn wagon way from the canal basin to Moreton in Marsh with a branch to Shipston on Stour. This bridge was constructed by prisoners from two Birmingham prisons, Wormwood Scrubs and Birmingham prison and was opened by H M The Queen Mother on 11th July 1964.

(Bridges are also mentioned in Joan's previous Volumes, Cameos: 16 , 74 and 75)

123. Stannalls Bridge (Wikipedia)

The formation of the old Cheltenham to Stratford main line between a point just to the south of Stratford and Long Marston, has been made into a cycleway. One of the spans of this impressive girder bridge is used for this purpose. The former down line span is used for the cycle way and the former up line span is disused and in very poor condition. Stannalls Bridge is linked to Stratford via the Greenway, a high quality surfaced path, suitable for cyclists, walkers and wheelchair users. It is part of the National Cycle Network, forming a five mile section of the West Midlands Cycle Route, which links Oxford to Derby via Birmingham. The Greenway is traffic free, but you cross some minor roads along the way into Stratford.

Stannalls Bridge.

124. Seven Meadows Road Bridge (Wikipedia)

The Seven Meadows Road Bridge was formerly a railway bridge and when the idea of another major road into Stratford was conceived, the rail bridge was incorporated and became the Seven Meadows Bridge. Motor traffic first crossed it in the late eighties/early nighties and is now known as the Stratford Southern Relief Road. The bridge crosses the River Avon at Lucy's Mill, to the south of Stratford. It stands on the site of Bridge 59 of the former Stratford and Midland Junction Railway and is supported by the piers of the original railway bridge.

125. Littleham Bridge (Wikipedia)

The parish of Alveston lies to the east of Stratford between the Avon River and the Banbury Road and is bounded on the west by Charlecote, Loxley and Alderminster. It was included in the borough of Stratford in 1924. Its present boundaries seem to be approximately those given in a Saxon charter of 985. The parish includes two separate villages of Alveston and Tiddington and part of the hamlet of Bridgetown, with the Manor House, which was once the residence of the Lanes and the Bishops. The main road from Stratford to Wellesbourne runs through Tiddington and there is a parallel road to the south, branching from Loxley Lane and going through Hunscote, which is described in 1669 as the road from Stratford to Southam, part of which is now private.

The Avon was crossed by a ferry at Alveston village and a ford near the Mill. Doddanford of 985. Lower down the stream opposite Cliffe Cottage is the probable site of Welcombe Ford, referred to in 1570. There is a single mention in 1658 of Alveston Bridge over the Avon, but its position cannot be identified.

An inquisition held at Coventry in 1417, exonerated the Priory of Worcester from the duty of repairing "Wroglow Brigge" in Alveston. This was probably the bridge which carries the Banbury Road over a small brook and the south eastern end of the parish which is marked as Rokesly Bridge on a map dated 1599. Littleham Bridge, where the Wellebsourne Road enters the parish of Charlecote, was the scene of a once celebrated murder (see 109) on 20 November 1820, when William Hiron, the farmer at Alveston Hill was attacked and killed near the spot by four men who were afterwards hanged at Warwick. The tradition is that the hole in which his head was found can never be filled.

126. The Holdings of the Bishop of Worcester

The Holdings of the Bishop of Worcester in the vicinity of Stratford, were divided into four manors; Hampton Lucy, Alveston (44 families), Stratford itself (29 families) and Loxley. The importance of this cameo is that at the time when the Domesday Book was written, Alveston had more families than Stratford.

Oligarchs managed the area and in 1835, the Municipal Corporation Act was passed, which led to elected Councils.

127. Suffragettes (Wikipedia)

Suffragettes were members of womens organisations in the late 19th and early 20th centuries, which advocated the extension of the franchise for women. It particularly refers to militants in Great Britain, such as members of the Women's Social and Political Union. Suffragettes wanted the right for women to vote. The move for women to have the vote really started in 1897 when

Millicent Fawcett founded the National Union of Women's Suffrage. Suffrage means the right to vote and that is what women wanted, hence its inclusion in Fawcett's title. Millicent Fawcett believed in peaceful protest. She felt that any violence or trouble would persuade men that women could not be trusted to have the right to vote. Her game plan was patience and logical arguments. Fawcett argued that women were allowed to hold responsible posts in society, such as sitting on school boards, but could not be trusted to vote. She argued that if Parliament made laws and if women had to obey these laws, then women should be part of the process of making the laws. She argued that as women had to pay taxes as men, they should have the same rights as men and one of her most powerful arguments was that wealthy mistresses of large manors and estates, employed gardeners, workmen, and labourers who could vote, but the women who employed them, could not.

However Fawcett's progress was very slow and she converted some of the members of the Labour Representation Committee (soon to become the Labour Party). Most men in Parliament believed that women simply would not understand how Parliament worked and therefore should not take part in the electoral process. This left many women angry and in 1903, the Women's Social and Political Union was formed by Emmeline Pankhurst and her daughters, Christabel and Sylvia. They wanted the women to have the right to vote. The Union became better known as the Suffragettes. Members of the Suffragettes were prepared to use violence to get what they wanted. Women won the right to vote in parliamentary elections in 1928.

Stratford itself was not without suffragists. A branch of the women's suffrage society was formed in the town in 1907, but it was a bi-election in the town held in 1909, that brought the question of women's rights to vote into focus. Suffragists were gathered under a yellow and black banner, bearing Shakespeare's most famous line "to be or not to be". Suffragette badges could be bought in the town and public meetings were held every day. The suffragettes ceased to campaign in the town on 23rd April and took part in the parade. On the following day, Christabel Pankhurst addressed two packed meetings in the town. From 1909 to 1913, suffragettes were regularly seen in Stratford at the time of the birthday celebrations. And there were other events. In the autumn of 1909, two plays were presented at the Corn Exchange entitled a Woman's Influence and How the Vote was Won.

In June 1913, Emily Davison was killed at Epsom Derby and just a month later, on 16 July, a march of 56 suffragettes from Carlisle to London, came through Stratford and passed through Birmingham. Before leaving, they held a public meeting in Rother Market.

128. Scotch Eggs (Silver Surfers)
Stratford's roads were designed to take horses and carts and journeys sometimes were quite long. The result of this was that the food had to be taken in the cart with the travellers and in 1738, Scotch Eggs were invented because they were pocket sized and were an ideal picnic for long journeys.

129. Emms Court
From a very early time, Sheep Street was the site of one of the town's markets. Around 1265, early deeds refer to

sales of land in the street where sheep are sold, but there is thus no mystery as to how the street got its name. The north side of Sheep Street was twice affected by the disastrous fires which swept Stratford in 1594, 1595 and 1614. On the first occasion, houses from the top of the street, down to the Shrieve's House, No 40, were affected, whilst in 1614, Shrieve's House may again have been destroyed as well as several houses further down the street on the same side. There is evidence of a fire on one of the newel posts, indicating that there had been fire in this house at some time. There is one important survival from the medieval time, namely No 3, with its jointed gable, a tiny building when compared with the others in the street. It is believed to date back to the 14th century and thus, to be the oldest domestic house still standing in the town.

A few of Sheep Street properties are still private houses and others have been converted into business premises recently. This residential character is very long-standing and was even more pronounced in the middle of the last century, when little clusters of labourers cottages were built in courts behind the main street frontage. The most notorious example was Emms Court, 10 or 11 tiny dwellings squeezed into the site behind No 12. These have long since been demolished but the passageway which gave access to them, can still be seen.

The large number of Sheep Street residents, over 300 in 1951 compared for example, with about 200 in High Street, many of them of the poorer sort, stimulated the opening of small taverns and beer houses. There were not many imposing establishments to be found in the main thoroughfares but the 'locals' like the Plough at No. 13, The Green Man at No. 19, and The Dog at No. 36, were examples of these. To put this into context, there is something similar which opened about two years ago in Greenhill Street, which is a little beer house called The Stratford Alehouse.

130. Consecrated Ground On Banbury Road

By chance, Joan had a phone call from a gentleman in a different county, saying that he was fascinated with stained glass and had bought a fragment of 15th century glass from a church now converted into two cottages on the Banbury Road. This fragment comes from a panel of stained glass that was in a church, situated on the Banbury Road, which has long since been converted

Fragment of stained glass window from 15th Century church on Banbury Road (which no longer exists).

into two cottages. The gentleman concerned, purchased it from Grainger Brown in Henley Street, opposite the Birthplace on June 19th 1964, for £15. (A note on the glass was written by hand and had been written by a previous purchaser). The successor to this little church when demolished, is the small church associated with St James and St John of Alveston, in Manor Road. The site of the church on Banbury Road can be seen on an ordnance survey map (old series) XLIV.7.

131. David Hutchings (Stratford-upon-Avon Canal)
As has been mentioned before, the Stratford-upon-Avon Canal was authorised by an initial Act of Parliament in 1793 and additional Acts in 1795 and 1799. Cutting began in November 1793 at Kings Norton on the Worcester and Birmingham Canal. The work progressed in various stages until the completed canal was opened at its junction with the River Avon on 24th June 1816.

The completed canal was 25 miles long and had cost £297,000 to build. The major construction on the canal included 56 locks and a 352 yard, 16 feet wide tunnel, a large single span brick aqueduct and three cast iron trough aqueducts, three high embankments and reservoirs, namely the Earlswood Lakes. (See Cameo 67) The lakes comprised of 25 acres of water, namely Engine Pool, Windmill Pool and Terry's Pool, which are situated close to Henley-in-Arden.

Freight on the canal increased to a peak in 1838 but with the coming of the railways this trade was gradually taken from the canal. The canal company sold out to Oxford Worcester and Wolverhampton Railway Company in 1856. Ownership passed to the G W Railway in 1865 and on to the State, on nationalisation in 1948. In 1964 there was a battle to prevent the closure of this canal. The Canal Society, in conjunction with the England Waterways Association and the Coventry Canal Society, interested the National Trust in acquiring the Southern Section of the canal for restoration. Mr David Hutchings who was known to Joan, was appointed Director of Operations and under his leadership, volunteers from various waterway societies, boy scouts, the armed services and later, prisoners from Winson Green Prison, carried out the restoration work from 1961 to 1964. The southern section was reopened to navigation on 11 July 1964 by Her Majesty the Queen Mother.

It is alleged that all this work was carried out under the leadership of Mr David Hutchings, who then sought planning permission to do so. After 11 years of negotiations, responsibility for the southern section was transferred to British Waterways on 1st April 1988 and is now owned by the Canal and River Trust.

132. The Swan Theatre (Focus Magazine)
The restoration of the Swan Theatre will be completed in time for the anniversary of William Shakespeare's death. It is expected that the world and his wife will come to Stratford in 2016, to celebrate the anniversary of one of the most remarkable playwrights in the world.

Work on the 4.5 million Swan Theatre Wing project, began in January 2014, to restore the façade and interior of the Grade II listed building, as well as to reveal the hidden heritage within the building and enhance the public spaces.

Built in 1879, the Swan Wing is the oldest part of the RSC's theatres, comprising of the exterior and front of house areas of the theatre in Waterside. The work has been so sensitively carried out that in many places, it is difficult to see where the building has been conserved in situ or a perfect colour match. The building was very dirty, picking up dirt through its life. It has been washed and steam cleaned very gently. It has been conservatively repaired and only renewed when essential.

The project has been supported by the Heritage Lottery Fund which awarded the theatre 2.8 million pounds along with the Garfield Weston Foundation and the Wolfson Foundation, and many other generous supporters. Leaded windows and gargoyles have been replaced exquisitely.

The distinctive wrap that featured in a life size photograph of the exterior of the Swan Theatre, was removed at the end of November 2015. The wrap was erected to hide the works that were happening to the exterior of the theatre, as well as to protect the trades people from the elements. It has now been taken away to be created into a unique merchandise, which will be sold to visitors to the theatre. Visitors can look forward to being able to buy a range of fashion bags, including a tote shopper, a back pack, a shoulder bag, a small and large flight bag, as well as a weekend sports grip.

2016 is going to be a very exciting year!

133. Arden Street's Victorian Properties
(Stratford-upon-Avon, Robert Bearman)

On the corner of Arden Street, was the Old Hospital, built in 1884, designed by the well known Edwardian architect, Edward Mountford. This building, one of the earliest in the town, to incorporate some Victorian half-timber construction, was to provide better facilities for the sick poor, who had previously been accommodated in a building in Chapel Lane. However, following its closure, this too, had been levelled to be replaced by the present hotel. As a token gesture towards conservation, the old clock tower was salvaged and placed on top of a new building. The stained glass window was rescued, with the help of Chris Ironmonger and Joan, and is now included in the chapel attached to the hospital. All that remains of the Victorian structure is what is known as the Gardener's Lodge, built in Arden Street in 1900. It still bears a plaque to the effect that it was built "in grateful acknowledgement of Mr Edward Corbett's generous legacy to this hospital".

The Victorian character of this part of the town has not been completely destroyed. On the opposite corner to the old hospital, Nos 2-7 Arden Street, built in 1866, as a private venture, are a very important survival.

At that time, the railway was a comparative newcomer to the area and the station, in its present form, had scarcely been built. But William Greener, merchant of Birmingham, and remembered by posterity as a innovatory gun manufacturer, had the idea of dragging Stratford into the 1860s by developing a suburb in Arden Street for would be for Birmingham commuters, built in the very latest style. Nos 2-7 Glencoe, were the result. The first of the few 19th century buildings in the town which represent what might be called the high Victorian manner. Gothic houses of this type with pointed windows and doorways and elaborate decorative brickwork, are fairly common in such places as Oxford. In Stratford, this row is virtually unique and a very important part of the town's architectural heritage, even though some original features have been lost. The architects were John H Hawkes and G F Hawkes of St Anne's Street, Birmingham.

The author's uncle was a director of Greeners the Gunsmiths and brother-in-law to her mother.

Housing of this type did not catch on and the next significant building operation was of a very different kind. A new company which combined concern, both for the moral and material welfare of the poor, with sound business sense, was to build cheap but respectable houses, which could then be let for low, but commercially viable rents. In this way, the town could rid itself of its slums and "do away with nursing beds of crime, pauperism and vice". By March 1877, 17 cottages had been built in Mansell Street, Nos 12-28, at right angles to Arden Street. By March the following year, another ten in Arden Street itself, Nos 8-17. This is an early example of housing provision for the poor. Beyond Mansell Street, there is a pleasant terrace of early Victorian houses, the earliest, No 25, built in the 1840s and the others, Nos 19, 21-24, from the 1960s and '70s. The name 'Foundry Court' applies to the modern infill between Nos 18 and 21, and refers to the large ironwork run by Ball Brothers, which flourished further down the street and has since been replaced with oversized office blocks.

134. Floods (Stratford Blog)

Stratford, being one of the lowest towns in the country, has always been subjected to floods. In fact, most of the outlying roads, such as Loxley, Tiddington and Warwick Road have been built on the flood plain. A marker on the wall of Waterside, shows the most disastrous flood levels. 2015 has been a memorable year for floods in all parts of the United Kingdom, it is important to note that

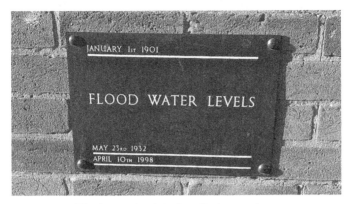

Flood water levels in Stratford-upon-Avon.

2015 has been no exception. It is certainly not unusual for the River Avon to flood. On the wall near the Royal Shakespeare theatre, are marks showing where the water has reached in exceptional floods over the past 100 years or so. The most recent mark is for the flood in 1998, when swans were seen to be floating down Waterside. The more recent flood in 2007 was not so high. The floods of 1932, just weeks after the opening of the Shakespeare Memorial Theatre, are also marked. The highest mark, some 30 cm above the others, commemorates the 1901 floods.

The worst flood in Stratford's history was that of September 1769, which coincided with the biggest and most heavily publicised event the town had seen. David Garrick's Shakespeare Jubilee will be described in detail in the next volume.

135. The Stratford-upon-Avon and Midland Junction Railway

(Arthur Jordan)

The origins of the Stratford-upon-Avon and Midland Junction Railway, are to be found in the Northampton and Banbury Railway, powers for which were granted by Parliament as early as 1847, although no line was open before 1866 and even then, it ran only from Blisworth on the London and North Western main line to Towcester, a distance of four miles. With its sights set on moving iron ore from Northamptonshire to South Wales, in 1866 this company changed its name to the Midland Counties and South Wales Railway, but in 1870, it realised that great difficulty would be experienced in even reaching Banbury. So, with a further name change, to Northampton and Banbury Junction Railway, it began service in June 1872 from Blisworth through Towcester, Wappenham and Helmdon, then over LNW metals from Cockley Brake Junction into Banbury station LNW. This line was worked with second hand engines from the LNW until 1875, when they were hired from that company, an arrangement which continued until the end of the N&B in 1910.

Another constituent of SMJ was the East and West Junction Railway, authorised in 1864, to link the Northampton and Banbury at Greens Norton (Towcester) with the GW Railway at Stratford-upon-Avon.

The GWR, as the Stratford-upon-Avon Railway, had reached the town by 1859, by a branch of single line, from Hatton Junction on the London to Birmingham line. The Oxford, Worcester and Wolverhampton Railway had struck northwards from Honeybourne, with a single line to reach Stratford-upon-Avon at the same time.

14 years later the East West Junction Railway sought an agreement for its trains to use the GWR station, when its line opened, but although a junction was installed, the East West own station was ready for departure of

the first train to run between Stratford-upon-Avon and Kineton on 1ˢᵗ July 1873. The Stratford Herald described the new station as "a... station", a small but substantially erected brick building, standing on land formerly known as Church Farm, Church Farm being what is now known as Seven Meadows Road. Part of the platform is still visible.

136. Easter (Social Media)

In 2016 Easter Sunday falls on 27ᵗʰ March while next year it will fall on 16 April and in 2018 it will be on 1ˢᵗ April. The Archbishop of Canterbury, the Most Revd Justin Welby, says he hopes to see Easter become a fixed date by the time he retires. His expectations could come to fruition in between five or ten years' time.

* * * *

Before Jayne and I begin Volume 5, I would like to acknowledge my publisher, who, like me, has taken no money from this compilation, to Gwilym Davies, I am most grateful.

Typing assistants!

VOLUME 5

Jayne and I are excited to be starting Volume 5, at the beginning of 2016, which promises to be a worldwide celebration of Shakespeare in Stratford-upon-Avon.

*   *   *   *   *

137. More On Easter

At present, Easter falls on the first Sunday following the first full moon after the vernal equinox around March 21st. This means it can fall on any Sunday between March 22nd and April 25th.

Easter Day in 2016 falls on 27th March.

138. The White Lion Inn (Henley Street)
(Shakespeare Birthplace Trust)

The White Lion Inn was first rebuilt in 1753 and there were two inns on this site for at least 75 years before that. The original White Lion is first mentioned in 1685, which joined the smaller inn, The Swan.

John Payton, realised the potential of these two inns, bought them both and modified them in the modern style. His modern inn filled the block between Henley Street and the Gild Pits (Guild Street). He bought much farm land behind the inn and when the Enclosure Act of 1774 was enacted, he was the largest landowner in the Welcombe and Bishopton Ward. Financial troubles started to beset him. Payton, together with George Alexander Stevens, the famous comic actor, discussed a Jubilee and negotiated with Garrick, the foremost actor at the time. The size of the Jubilee arrangements overtook John Payton, which meant he could not offer accommodation to his regular guests. His bedrooms were named after Shakespeare's famous characters. John Payton died in 1780 and as the business was struggling, he had to seek £500 to pay off his debts. The debts remained outstanding until the inn was sold. Payton had overreached himself.

The reputation of the inn was unimpaired, even leading to other inns in the town, the Red Horse and The Shakespeare, but once sold, The White Lion was not allowed to name the rooms as before. The reason for its popularity, was that Henley Street and the White Lion were on the main post chaise route from London to Holyhead. His son, John, was mayor three times and did not take a liking to being an innkeeper and so involved himself in the life of Stratford.

Whilst in Shakespeare Birthplace Trust reading room, Joan poured through two files of public houses in Stratford. According to Malcolm Rouch, well known restaurateur in Stratford during the 1970s and 1980s, one could not become an innkeeper without being married.

139. Reginald "Rex" Warneford
(The Stratfordian – King Edward VI School Magazine)
Born in India on 18 October 1891, Reginald Arthur John Warneford's formative years saw him receive an unconventional education with his father, a railway engineer, riding engine footplates – throwing logs into the firebox and pulling the whistle cord. He went on a tiger hunt, rode a pony, studied the stars and learnt native dialects and the law of the jungle.

It was a wonderful life for a boy. In 1900, Rex was sent alone to England to live with his paternal grandfather, Tom Warneford. His grandfather was a great friend of the headmaster, Cornwell Robertson, so in January 1901, Rex arrived at King Edward VI school, as a choral scholar and boarded in the school house in Chapel Lane, that stood where the car park is today.

Cornwell Robertson believed that it was not the sole object of the school, to cram a boy and stuff as much learning into him, as it could. He liked to see a boy work, whatever he was doing, not with his head alone, but with his heart as well.

Rex was very happy at school and felt secure. He excelled at anything he could do with his hands, such as carpentry, physics, engineering and he also had an appetite for mathematics.

The First World War interrupted his education. Rex passed a stiff test and was assessed for 'above average intelligence, iron nerves and initiative'. He joined Number One Squadron and RMAS, flying a Morane-Saulnier monoplane, with instructions to carry out patrols, to bomb submarine bases and German troop concentrations in Belgium.

Rex was shot down and only his safety harness saved him from being thrown out. He managed to land, despite a fuel pipe being broken, 30 miles behind enemy lines, where he managed to repair the damage, using a handkerchief and a cigarette holder. He took off again, just as he was spotted by a German cavalry patrol. Arriving back at the base at St Pol, he made a brief report and fell asleep for eight hours. When he awoke, he was told that news of his destruction of a Zeppelin, his bravery and individual daring had flashed around the world. King George V sent a telegram awarding Rex the Victoria Cross and the French President made him a Chevalier de la Legion d'Honneur with the automatic companion of the Croix de Guerre.

Only two weeks later, he was ordered to return to duty and to test a new Farman F27 biplane. During the flight, the propeller broke off and cut away the tail of the machine, sending the plane into an uncontrollable spin. 700 feet below, it turned upside down and Rex died from his injuries. He was 23 years old.

140. The Old Ferry House (Southern Lane)
(Wikipedia)

The Old Ferry House was listed on 9 February 1972 as a Grade 2 listed building. It is a typical Georgian townhouse, built between 1792 and 1794.

It was built for Edward Easthope, as a private residence, but has been subsequently used by the Royal Shakespeare Theatre for their visiting actors. Joan frequently met Griffith Jones on a Sunday morning at the newspaper stall on the pavement, outside what is now the Old Red Lion Court.

141. Sir William Dugdale, Second Baronet CBE, MC, DL
(22 March 1922 – 13 November 2014)

High Steward for Stratford-upon-Avon from 1976 to 2014.

Sir William has been mentioned in a previous cameo No: 47. The role of High Steward is largely ceremonial now.

From the dates above, it is sad to note that Sir William died just over a year ago. On Monday 29th

February 2016, the Marquis of Hertford was installed as the new High Steward, a lifetime appointment.

142. Tourism (Roger Pringle)

Stratford was on many coaching routes, over which the post chaise passed. The carriages travelled a long, long way and so many changes of horses were needed. 1830 was the height of the stage coach era and there were five key inns, most of which were in Henley Street, because as previously mentioned, Stratford was on the coaching route from London to Holyhead. Each coach had a name and to name but a few, there was the Union, the Ocdonia Express, the Aurora and the Rocket.

In 1817, 24 coaches a day passed through Stratford. In 1709/10, Shakespeare published a pocket sized tourist guide. In 1709, the plays that were being performed were listed and a first attempt was made at a biography. The White Lion in Henley Street was the famous coaching inn and Mr Payton was the proprietor (See Cameo No: 138). All the important visitors always stayed there. Washington Irvine was one of his most famous guests.

Survey maps began to appear in 1765 and in 1799, Ronald Freeman, who was an apothecary in the town, wrote the first guidebook. In 1814 a second guidebook by R T Wheeler was published and in 1824, a short book about Shakespeare's Birthplace, followed in 1826 by a little book about the horse drawn tram.

143. Warwick House (Birmingham Road)

This well-known building on stilts has been on the corner of Clopton Road and Birmingham Road for many years and has had several uses. At the beginning of 2016, Stratford Town Trust decided to sell it, but keeping the freehold. It was sold eventually to Orbit Housing. During the initial consultations, Orbit chose a name of the new building, that is to be erected on the site and it was to be Merchants House. Joan being a member of the Trust and a lover of Stratford, suggested to the Board of Trustees, that we ask Orbit to change the name to Fordham House. Edward Fordham, in 1831, began his brewery business, on the opposite corner, the site of the Maltings in Brewery Street. On the aforementioned corner, was the cooperage, run by James Cox in partnership with Edward Fordham Flower. In 1831 the business that Edward Flower and James Cox had started, was divided. James Cox was a religious man, who built an elegant chapel in Payton Street for the Baptist congregation. In 1832, James Cox began a ragged school in Sheep Street for 40 scholars.

The demolition of Warwick House began on Thursday 11 February 2016, to make way for a brand new residential development, bringing key worker accommodation to the heart of the town. The new building will consist of 82 private rental high quality apartments, due for completion in the summer of

Fordham House.

2017. Being so close to the hospital and town centre, the apartments will be targeted at local, key workers. Preference for the 64 one bedroom and 18 two bedroom apartments, will be let to those such as health and emergency service workers and teachers, as well as local people. The new homes are to be let on an assured, shorthold tenancy.

The Orbit Group is one of the largest housing organisations in the country and is listed as one of the top five landlords in the UK by Sector Magazine 24 Housing. It has been constructed by the Deeley Group based in Coventry.

(Text attributed to Derrick Smart)

In 1831, Edward Flower and James Cox, having opened the brewery, were responsible for cooperage making, which were wooden beer casks, known as hogsheads (54 gallons), barrels (36 gallons), kilderkins (18 gallons), firkins (9 gallons) and pins (4½ gallons). These casks and their manufacture were dependent on the sales of ales produced by the brewery on its formation and later, in better times. As James Cox was a timber merchant, this fitted very well with Edward Flower's ability to be a brewer. Progress was slow in the early days and the Brewery struggled to make ends meet.

This obstacle was overcome, when it was decided to purchase local inns, as sales outlets for their beer. Most inns in those days, brewed their own beer on the premises. As mentioned before, in 1852, a much larger brewery was built and sales and brewing quantities became a larger enterprise. A tunnel was built under Clopton Road with a track laid to move the casks from the cooperage to the Brewery site. The outline of this tunnel is still visible on the entrance to Clopton Court flats to Clopton Court Road.

The street which is now called Brewery Street, used to be called Navigation Street, owing to its proximity to the canal and the One Elm wharf. The railway, as previously mentioned, arrived in the town from the south in 1859, with a single, broad-gauge and standard-gauge line from Honeybourne junction. This gave access to Oxford and London, as well as the West Country. It connected with Worcester and Birmingham and its environs. This firstly terminated in Old Town (known as Sanctus Street today). The operators were the Oxford, Worcester and Wolverhampton Railway, the forerunners of the Great Western Railway. It later, in 1863, moved to the Alcester Road, the present location of Stratford-upon-Avon Railway Station.

This was followed by another railway line from the north in 1860. This line was of mixed broad-gauge and standard-gauge, and terminated on the Birmingham Road, the present Wharf Road area, under the umbrella of the GWR. In 1863, both lines terminated on the Alcester Road, extra rail track was laid for the link-up, with the Birmingham Road site being turned into a goods only terminus and a coal wharf.

144. The Flower Family (Wikipedia)

There can be no doubt about the influence the Flower Family has had on the evolution of Stratford-upon-Avon since 1831 when the brewery was founded by Edward Fordham Flower.

Richard Flower a brewer, a banker, a politician and sheep breeder of Marden Hill, was despondent about the future of agriculture in Warwickshire. He emigrated to America with his entire family and to make this a possibility, Richard hired two ships to take him and his entourage, goods and chattels to America, from Liverpool.

Edward, his youngest son was twelve years old when the family left in 1817. On arrival Edward helped his father establish a new home. In America, Edward became known as a remarkably energetic character. When he was nineteen years old Edward became very ill and was determined to return home. Formal education had not been possible in America and on his return he stayed with a Robert Owen in Lanark. It is not clear how he came to Warwickshire; however in 1827 he married Celina Greaves of Barford. Edward had married into a wealthy family but remained independent by going into business on his own and gained experience in brewing through relatives. The Fordham family had a business in Hertfordshire and it was here he served his apprenticeship, when he returned from America.

With a legacy from his father Richard who had recently died in Illinois, he established his own brewery on the land between the Birmingham and Clopton Roads. The brewery was served by a canal wharf which facilitated the delivery of materials along with the onward distribution of finished products.

Early years were difficult but with the introduction of East India Pale Ale based on the Pale Ales of Burton on Trent, put the brewery on the map.

In 1852 Edward was joined by Charles his son and later by another son Edgar. The company expanded and a new brewery was built nearby. The site of this new building was the cooperage and the main brewery was on the opposite corner. The brewery expanded still further in 1874 when a new building was built situated west of the Birmingham Road close to the station and was served by its railway sidings and by electricity.

Edward retired in 1863 having built a mansion house at the top of Welcombe Road, the house remains and is called The Hill. Edward was four times Mayor and he was also a Magistrate. He oversaw the Shakespeare Birthday celebrations and stood for Parliament twice but was unsuccessful both times. He and Celina moved to London where he became a philanthropist, in particular in the field of equine care. He died at his home in Hyde Park Gardens in 1883.

Charles, his son also served as Mayor and lived at Avonbank in Southern Lane with Sarah, his wife. Following Charles' death she carried on his good work by funding the restoration of the King Edward VI Grammar School, the Alms Houses and the Guild Chapel. Sarah died in 1908, her generosity knew no bounds and her garden is still in use today.

Barges at Flowers Brewery.

The brewery, by this time, was the town's main employer with a workforce of 200 people. The Company owned 20 Public Houses. Edgar's sons Archibald and Richard became directors.

Charles owned large tracts of land and in 1875, he donated a two acre site and launched an international campaign to open a theatre to commemorate Shakespeare's life. The new theatre opened in 1879 with a performance of Much Ado about Nothing. This theatre was destroyed by fire in 1926. Edward's nephew Archibald, launched a campaign for a replacement, raising millions of dollars in the United States of America. On a recent visit to the theatre, Joan and her daughter, Sheena, found themselves sitting underneath the very large plaque positioned on the wall, commissioned to commemorate Archibald's benefaction.

The Elisabeth Scott Theatre opened in Stratford-upon-Avon, this was the first important public building in Britain to be designed by a female architect. In July 1929 the foundation stone was laid with Masonic ritual, and was reopened in 1932. The Masonic ceremonies around the foundation stone, paled into insignificance besides the folderol of the official opening on 23rd April 1932, broadcast and relayed live to the United States (from whence came most of the funding). Some 100,000 people came to see the Prince of Wales arrive by monoplane (self-piloted), to declare the building open, receive a key from Scott – a modern figure in her cloche hat and neatly cropped hair – and attend part of the opening production of Henry IV and then fly off again, well before the end of the performance.

Orbit Housing is proud to name their new building Fordham House in recognition of the contribution made by the remarkable Flower family, and the part the family has played in the evolution of Stratford-upon-Avon. Flowers Ales still exist but their production has been transferred to Whitbread's Brewery in Cheltenham.

145. James Cox (Timber Merchant)
(SBT Archives)

On 24th June 1874, James Cox the younger (timber merchant), was an executor with Frederick Vincent Martin, plumber and glazier, to a will. In the will, was mentioned a piece of land on the Shipston Road. On 31 December 1885, James Cox and Robert Cort Cox went into partnership. On 24 December 1890, there was a supplementary agreement, altering their partnership, the profits thereof, dividing them three quarters to a quarter,(four fifths to a fifth) to James and Robert Cort Cox. The executors were told that James Cox wished to take the business under the terms provided for and to purchase the property known as Avon Bridge Wharf, together with the saw mill.

Joan read in the Shakespeare Birthplace archives that Robert Cort Cox had mortgaged Eastnor House (his home) and the rights of way on the adjoining private road, in 1917. He made a gift of furniture to Jessie Margaret Cox, his wife. The house had previously belonged to Mr John Greenway and had been let to the Reverend F W Aston.

Notes from the 1861 Census
Robert Cort Cox 1858 (Timber Merchant)

James Cox, the elder, in 1858, had a wife called Ann and in the Census they are down as living in Old Stratford, which was part of Stratford town, and included Bridgetown. James Cox had nine children, some of which were Ann's by a previous marriage. At this time he was 36 and his wife was 34. Ann A C Cox was 12, Mary Alomia was 10, Jane B B Cox was 9. The youngest was Robert Cort Cox who was 3. Date of death of Robert Cort Cox was June 1943. James Cox also owned a house called Cedar Villa on the Warwick Road.

James Cox's wife had been married before and on 10 April 1841, James Cox leased land from Joseph Holton and then built a quay and walls, which were in existence for 35 years, at a rent of £5 per annum. On 31st October 1866, James contracted to purchase a wharf for £60 and on 24th November 1866, there was a licence to assign premises to James Cox. On 28 June 1916, James having died, Joan saw an entry regarding James Cox's will, where he left the residue to Lawrence Web Cox and Jessie Margaret Cox, the wife of Robert Cort Cox, who both received certificates. Mary Monica Cox received shares, she lived in Mayfield Avenue in 1895. In 1942, there were entries regarding gifts to Robert Cort Cox and wife, Jessie Margaret Cox.

Coal was the principal commodity with no less than 14 coal wharfs on the Bank Croft area and by 1851, there were two timber wharfs, a stone wharf and a lead and glass wharf. There were two dry docks, managed by boat builder, Thomas Kemp and a timber business, established by James Cox in 1839.

This whole area was transformed in little more than a decade, from scrubland to a thriving, commercial centre.

(Taken from Stratford-upon-Avon, a History of its Streets and Buildings), Page 68, Bob Bearman).

Hutchings Coal Wharf.

The commercial area thrived until the arrival of the railway, when very few of the businesses could be sustained. The Bank Croft became the Bancroft, which was the beginning of its rejuvenation into a recreational area.

Edward Flower was 19 when he came back to England from America. He married Celina from Barford and bought his first house in Payton Street. His first joint business with James Cox, as a timber merchant, was in the wharfs behind the One Elm pub.

Richard, his father had two friends in Hertfordshire, Edward King Fordham and John Fordham. They formed a partnership and opened a bank in Royston. The Fordhams were brewers. The Royston bank was called Fordham Flower and Co. In 1825 control passed to the Fordhams and became Fordham & Co. The Fordhams lost control when it merged with other banks and became Barclays and Co, now known as Barclays!

146. A Shot

Many of the public houses in Stratford sell shots in small glasses. You may have wondered where the name came from. In America, in the pubs in the west, many of the cowboys could not afford to pay for a glass of wine, so they paid for it with a bullet.

147. Name In Print

It has been one of Joan's long time ambitions to get a letter accepted by one of the national newspapers. This, she succeeded in doing, at the end of 2015. She wrote to the Editor, stating that during the height of the bombing of England during the Second World War, the Houses of Parliament were to be moved to Stratford-upon-Avon, the theatres being the venue for both the House of Lords and House of Commons. Luckily, this never came about, but the letter was printed (An Architectural History by Marian J Pringle).

148. Arden Hotel

(Sarah Flower, widow of Charles Flower)

When Charles Flower died, Sarah Flower became a philanthropist in his place. There were no houses on the town side of Stratford in 1908, as this land belonged to the late Mrs Sarah Flower.

Map of land belonging to the late Mrs Sarah Flower on Waterside.

In the 16th Century there were only 1,500 people living in Stratford. The main house of what is now the Arden Hotel, is called Udimor House which has been standing there from the late to mid-17th Century. Even before that, in the 16th Century, Brooke House stood in this position. The foundations were owned by John Shakespeare and William allegedly wrote some works in the garden. An Elizabethan knot garden would have been found on this site during William Shakespeare's life.

149. The Bear and Ragged Staff Arms
(The Coate of Arms of Warwickshire)
(Wikipedia)

Meaning: Gules, a Bear erect Argent, muzzled of the first collard and chained or supporting a ragged staff of the second, the chai reflexed over the back and encircling the staff on a chief of the third three cross-crosslets of the first. The shield ensigned with ural crown gold. Motto 'NON SANZ DROICT' not without right. Granted 7th July 1931.

The Bear and Ragged Staff have long been associated with Warwickshire. The origins of these emblems are lost in the distant past, but have been associated with the Earls of Warwick since at least as early as the 14th Century. William Dugdale, in the 17th Century, recalls that the legendary Arthgallus and British Earl of Warwick, and Knight of King Arthur's Round Table, thought that his name came from the Welsh artos or bear. He also suggested that the ragged staff was chosen because Morvidus, Earl of Warwick, killed a giant with a broken branch of a tree. These claims cannot be supported and Dugdale was just recalling medieval legends. However, there is no doubt that the bear and ragged staff were first used by the Beauchamp family, who became Earls of Warwick in 1268, as a badge or mark of identity in addition to their own Coat of Arms.

At first the emblems seem to have been used independently. In 1387, Thomas Beauchamp II (Earl from 1369 to 1402) owned a bed of black material embroidered with a golden bear and silver staff, which is the earliest known occurrence of the two emblems together. The bear and ragged staff have been used by subsequent holders of the Earldom of Warwick, the Dudleys and the Grevilles and are borne as a crest by the present Earl. Over the centuries they have also come to be associated with the county and used as a badge by the 1st Warwickshire Militia regiment and the Warwickshire Constabulary. Warwickshire County Council obtained permission to adopt the bear and ragged staff for their common seal in 1907. The three cross-crosslets are taken from the arms of the Beauchamps, who were earls of Warwick from 1268 to 1449. They are perhaps the most famous of all the families which have held the earldom of Warwick and this together with the world-wide fame of the Beauchamp Chapel in St Mary's Church in Warwick, makes the inclusion of their arms in the county's armorial bearings, particularly appropriate. The motto, in Norman-French, is that of William Shakespeare, without doubt, the county's most famous son.

150. Changes In Stratford In 2016

As I was getting up this morning on 25th February 2016, I decided that Jayne and I could be writing this book for ever. The things that we write about have not been written about before, because some of them have not even happened!

I was getting ready to go to Coventry, there was a picture on television of the Flying Scotsman arriving at Kings Cross Station in London for the first time in many decades. Continuing on the theme of making history, the Toll House on Clopton Bridge is to be transformed very shortly, New Place is in the process of being transformed in preparation for Shakespeare's

Artist's impression of Bell Court.

anniversary in April, the Guild Chapel is having a lot of work carried out. The Guild Hall adjacent to the Guild Chapel, where the original Town Council used to meet, has been completely renovated, in order that the public can gain access. Warwick House on the Birmingham Road has almost been eliminated, in preparation for the emergence of a new building to be called Fordham House. There is to be a new hotel in Rother Street on the site that used to be the home of a hotel. In the meantime, it has had many uses, including the home of the CAB and the Registry Office.

Plan of new development

Another enormous change to Stratford town centre is the emerging Bell Court, where the curfew bell, which has been in storage, is to be reinstated. All this in one year, is an immense change that Stratford will soon become used to.

151. The Gift of a Statue to Stratford

On Tuesday 23rd February 2016, Joan was invited to the unveiling of a new sculpture of William Shakespeare in its new, permanent home on the Bancroft Gardens. Lawrence Holofcener, American sculptor and former actor and lyricist, gifted this bronze sculpture of a young William Shakespeare. Mr Holofcener was 90 years old on that Tuesday and had already made his name in England with another permanent sculpture in Bond Street in London. All Lawrence's sculptures can be interacted with, as they are all connected with a bench.

Following the unveiling, the theatre invited my daughter and me into the restaurant for a cup of tea, where Lawrence was presented with a birthday cake.

The statue of William Shakespeare gifted to Stratford by Lawrence Holofcener. The sculpture is situated in the Bancroft Gardens.

Mr. Lawrence Holofcener poses alongside his statue at its unveiling.

152. Ditty Number Two

As taught to Joan by her father

> *On Monday I had bread and dripping*
> *On Tuesday I had dripping and bread*
> *On Wednesday and Thursday I had dripping and*
> *   toast but that's only dripping and bread*
> *On Friday I called for the landlord and asked him*
> *   for a change*
> *So on Saturday morning, just for a change, I had*
> *   dripping without any bread*

153. Secretary

In Shakespeare's time, very few people could read and write and only with your very closest friends, could you share your most important documents. These close friends had to share a secret and that is where the name 'Secretary' comes from, somebody with whom you could share your secrets.

154. Stratfords of the World (Formerly Sister Cities)
During Joan's time on the Town Council, she met many interesting people, including Ted Lloyd, who was Mayor at the time (1989-90). During his mayoralty, some Stratford musicians and actors travelled to Connecticut in the United States, where two large cities had already formed a bond. Stratford joined these two cities and Sister Cities was chosen as a name because of this unusual relationship. Joan became Chairman of this group before its name was changed.

Rather than try to explain what happened next, I am taking an excerpt from a web page of Stratfords of the Worlds, the Society's present name, written by Dr Geoffrey Lees who puts it more succinctly.

A brief history of Stratfords of the World
Stratfords of the World (formerly known as Stratford-upon-Avon Sister Cities – a brief history by Dr. Geoffrey Lees, former Mayor of Stratford-upon-Avon).

Since the mid 1980s Stratford-upon-Avon has been privileged to enjoy a Sister Cities link with other Stratfords of the world following an invitation from Stratford Connecticut and Stratford Ontario to establish exchanges between the three communities. The link has subsequently been extended to include Stratford New Zealand, Stratford Prince Edward Island and Stratford Victoria (Australia).

The first visit was in April 1984 when the Stratford Connecticut High School Band visited Stratford Ontario. The following spring the Connecticut Band toured England performing in Stratford-upon-Avon during the Shakespeare Birthday Celebrations along with the Perth County Pipe Band from Ontario and the

Stratford-upon-Avon Wind Band Association. This was the beginning of the three way link between Stratfords of the old world and the new world.

In July 1986 Connecticut became host to visitors from Stratford residents of Ontario and the United Kingdom. This reunion was followed by others, again with a mainly musical theme, in Stratford (UK) in 1987, Stratford (Ontario) in 1988 and Stratford (Ct again) in 1997.

In the following years the opportunity presented itself to include drama, dance and other cultural activities into the objectives of the Sister City link, a highlight occurring during summer of 1991 when a group of actors from Stratford Connecticut came to England to present a play entitled "Stratford Characters" written by Steven Otfinoski. The People of Stratford Drama group from Stratford UK contributed a piece written by local author Charles Calvert.

Two years later in 1993 the 'People of Stratford' joined with the 'English Renaissance Dancers' in a week-long visit to Stratford Connecticut. As reported in the Connecticut 'Stratford Star', "the two groups presented a series of programmes celebrating and re-creating the life, times and works of Shakespeare, using dance, music and, of course, his own words".

Reunions have continued at approximately two year intervals e.g. UK 1992, Ontario 1993, Connecticut 1995. In 1997 the enlargement of the world Stratford grouping saw visitors from Stratford New Zealand and Stratford Prince Edward Island join their hosts in Warwickshire, with New Zealand taking up the challenge to host the next reunion in 1999, this time with Stratfordians from Victoria, Australia taking part.

Since that time, during which the organisation adopted a new title of "Stratfords of the World", reunions have flourished, taking place in Prince Edward Island (2001), Victoria (2003), UK (2005), Ontario (2007), Taranaki (2010), Prince Edward Island (2012) and Connecticut in 2014. This year, 2016, Stratford-upon-Avon is once again the host. Approximately 150 guests from the other Stratfords will be descending on our small town anytime soon.

155. Old Parish Names

Saxon names for parts of Stratford-upon-Avon have sometimes remained intact, but not always. Ruin Clifford (Clifford Chambers) extended along the left bank of the Avon, from the Stour to Mycel Straet, which was a Roman Road, now called the Banbury Road. It formed the south west border of Alveston. Bishopton, the north west of Stratford, is described in 1016 as lying between Shottery and Clopton. Its boundaries were Sealstret (Alcester Road) and Feldene Stret, now the Birmingham Road. Its third boundary was Shottery Brook.

The reason that Holy Trinity Church is away from the centre of Stratford and remote, is that it occupies the site of a Saxon monastery. Until 1879, this part of the town was outside the borough. There was confusion since 1591, of the difference between the parish boundary and the borough boundary as both institutions were liable to pay money by the County Justices. This problem was presented to the Judges of Assize, in 1628, who found it difficult and doubtful.

Stratford takes its name from the crossing of the Avon by a Roman road which ran from the Ryknield Street at

Alcester to join the Fosse. The settlement at this point, developed into the borough of Stratford-upon-Avon, and Old Stratford comprised also the hamlets of Shottery, Luddington, Dodwell, Drayton, Bishopton, Clopton, Welcombe and Bridgetown, besides the isolated hamlet of Bushwood. This large area represents the estate held as early as the 7th Century, by the church of Worcester, and its boundaries can at some points, be identified in the charters of the Saxon bishops.

The present boundaries were formed by the local Government Act of 1894, and have been changed several times since. To solve this problem, once and for all, 1,000 elm trees were planted on the boundary, together with 40 ash trees. The last ash tree was cut down and sold in 1847. The last elm tree stood on the land at the corner of Clopton Road and Birmingham Road, now the site of the new Fordham House, and was removed when Warwick House was built.

156. Pragnells

George Pragnell is a third generation family run jewellers in the heart of Stratford. Its workshop uses gemstones from Columbian emeralds to Kashmir sapphires and antique and period jewellery. The shop is housed within the walls of a 16th Century building within a stone's throw of Shakespeare's birthplace. Joan's grandfather was one of the first jewellers in Birmingham, before the advent of motorcars. He was one of the suppliers of rings to George Pragnell in the 1930s. In fact, he was one of the first gentlemen of Birmingham to own a car, when, because they were horseless carriages, someone had to walk in front with a red flag. The business was in the heart of the jewellery quarter and three of his sons, of which Joan's father was the youngest, took part in the manufacture of jewellery. Following the Second World War, having been annexed by the Ministry of Defence to make parts for aircraft engines, it reverted to making jewellery once the war had ended. One of Arthur Walter Crosbee & Sons' customers was George Pragnell, as mentioned above.

157. Shakespeare's Will

(Extracted in its original form from Wikipedia)

This had a very rare public outing on 7th December 2015 in the Shakespeare Birthplace Trust during a public exhibition.

"Testamentum Willemi Shackspeare Registretur

In the name of god Amen I William Shackspeare of Stratford-upon-Avon in the countrie of Warr' gent in perfect health and memorie god by praysed doe make and Ordayne this my last will and testament in manner and forme followeing that ys to saye first I Comend my Soule into the hands of god my Creator hoping and assuredlie beleeving through thonelie merittes of Jesus Christe my Saviour to be made partaker of lyfe everlastinge And my bodye to the Earthe whereof yt ys made.

Item I Gyve and bequeath unto my sonne in Law and Daughter Judyth One Hundred and fyftie pounds of lawfull English money to be paied unto her in manner and forme following That ys to saye One Hundred Poundes in discharge of her marriage porcion within one yeare after my deceas with consideracion after the Rate of twoe shillinges in the pound for soe long tyme as the same shalbe unpaid unto her after my deceas & the fyftie pounds Residewe therof upon her surrendering of or gyving of such sufficient securitie as the overseers of this my will shall like of to Surrender or graunte All her estate and Right that shall discend or come unto her after my deceas or that she nowe hath of in or to one Copiehold tenemente with the appertenances lyeing & being in Stratford-upon-Avon aforesaied in the saide countie of warr' being parcell or holden of the mannor of Rowington unto my daughter Susanna Hall and her heires for ever.

Item I gyve and bequeath unto my saied Daughter Judyth One Hundred and ffyftie Poundes more if shee or Anie issue of her bodie Lyvinge att the end of three yeares next ensueing the daie of the date of this my will during which tyme my executors to paie her consideracion from my deceas according to the Rate afore saied. And if she dye within the saied terme without issue of her bodye then my will ys and and I doe gyve and bequeath One Hundred Poundes therof to my Neece Eliabeth Hall and ffiftie Poundes to be sett fourth by my executors during the lief of my Sister Johane Harte and the use and proffitt therof cominge shalbe payed to my saied Sister Jone and after her deceas the saied L li shall Remaine Amongst the childredn of my saied Sister Equallie to be devided Amongst them. But if my saied daughter Judith be lyving att the end of the saeid three yeares or anie issue of her bodye then my will ys and soe I devise and bequeath the saied Hundred and ffyftie poundes to be sett out by my executors and overseers for the best benefit of her and her issue and the stock not to be paied unto her soe long as she shalbe marryed and Covert Baron by my executors and overseers but my will ys that she shall have the consideracion yearelie paied unto her during her lief and after her deceas the saied stock and condieracion to bee paid to her children if she have Anie and if not to

144

her executors or Assignes she lyving the saied terme after my deceas provided that if such husbond as she shall att thend of the saied three yeares by marryed unto or attain after doe sufficiently Assure unto her and thissue of her bodie landes answereable to the portion gyven unto her and to be adjudged soe by my executors and overseers then my will ys that the saied CL li shalbe paied to such husbond as shall make such assurance to his owne use.

Item I gyve and bequeath unto my saied sister Jone XX li and all my wearing Apprell to be paied and delivered within one yeare after my deceas. And I doe will and devise unto her the house with the appurtenances in Stratford where in she dwelleth for her naturall lief under the yearelie Rent of xiid.

Item I gyve and bequeath unto her three sonnes William Hart—Hart and Michaell Harte ffyve pounds A peece to be payed within one yeare after my decease to be sett out for her within one yeare after my deceas by my executors with thadvise and direccons of my overseers for her best proffitt untill her marriage and then the same with the increase thereof to be paied unto her.

Item I gyve and bequath unto her the said Elizabeth Hall All my Plate (except my brod silver and gilt bole) that I now have att the date of this my will.

Item I gyve and bequeath unto the Poore of Stratford aforesaied tenn poundes; to Mr Thomas Combe my Sword; to Thomas Russell Esquier ffyve poundes and to ffrauncis collins of the Borough of Warr' in the countie of Warr' gent. thriteene poundes Sixe shillinges and Eight pence to be paied within one yeare after my deceas.

Item I gyve and bequeath to mr richard Hamlett Sadler Tyler thelder XXVIs VIIId to buy him A Ringe;

to William Raynoldes gent XXVIs VIIId to buy him a Ringe; to my godson William Walker XXVIs VIIId in gold and to my ffellowes John Hemynges, Richard Burbage and Heny Cundell XXVIs VIIId A peece to buy them Ringes.

Item I Gyve Will Bequeth and Devise unto my Daughter Susanna Hall for better enabling of her to performe this my will and towardes the performans thereof All that Capitall Messuage or tenemente with the appertenaces in Stratford aforesaid called the newe plase wherein I now Dwell and two messuags or tenementes with the appurtenances scituat lyeing and being in Henley Streete within the borough of Stratford aforesaied. And all my barnes, stables, Orchardes, gardens, landes, tenementes and herediaments whatsoever scituat lyeing and being or to be had receyved, perceyved or taken within the townes and Hamletts, villages, ffieldes and groundes of Stratford-upon-Avon, Old Stratford, Bushopton and Welcombe or in anie of them in the saied countie of warr And alsoe All that Messuage or tenemente with thappurtenances wherein one John Robinson dwelleth, scituat, lyeing and being in the blackfriers in London nere the Wardrobe and all other my landes tenementes and hereditamentes whatsoever. To Have and to hold All and singular the saied premisses with their Appurtenances unto the saied Susanna Hall for and during the terme of her naturall lief and after her deceas to the first sonne of her bodie lawfullie yssueing and to the heiries Males of the bodie of the saied Second Sonne lawfullie yssyeinge and for defalt of such heires Males of the bodie of the saied third sonne lawfullie yssye ing And for defalt of such issue the same soe to be Reamine to the ffourth sonne, ffythe, sixte and seaventh sonnes of her bodie lawfullie issueing one after Another and to the heires Males of the bodies of the saied ffourth, ffythe, Sixte and Seaventh sonnes lawfullie yssueing in such mamer as yt ys before Lymitted to be and remaine to the first, second and third Sonns of her bodie and to their heires males. And for defalt of such issue the saied premisses to be and Remaine to my sayed Neede Hall and the heires Males of her bodie Lawfully yssueing for default of... such issue to my daughter Judith and the heires of me the saied William Sahckspere for ever.

Item I gyve unto my wief my second best bed with the furniture; Item I gyve and bequeath to my saied daughter Judith my broad silver gilt bole.

All the rest of my goodes Chattels, Leases, plate, jewles and Household stuffe whatsoever after my dettes and Legasies paied and my funerall expences discharged, I gyve devise and bequeath to my Sonne in Lawe John Hall gent and my daughter Susanna his wief whom I ordaine and make executors of this my Last will and testament. And I doe intreat and Appoint the saied Thomas Russell Esquier and ffrauncis Collins gent to be overseers herof And doe Revoke All former wills and publishe this to be my last will and testament. In witnes whereof I have hereunto put my Seale hand the Daie and Yeare first above Written.

Witness to the publishing hereof: Fra: Collyns, Juilyus Shawe, John Robinson, Hamnet Sadler, robert Whattcott.

By me William Shakespeare

Probatum coram Magistro Williamo Byrde legum doctore Commissario etc xxiido die mensis Junii Anno domini 1616 Juramento Jahannis Hall unius executorum etc. Cui etc de bene etc Jurati Reservata potestate etc Sussane Hall alteri executorum etc cum venerit etc petitur.

Inventarium exhibitum."

158. Shrieve's House (40 Sheep Street)
(The real home of John Falstaff)
(As given to Joan by Janet Ford, present incumbent)

William Shrieve, the Sheriff, the first extant leaser of 1542, the house, at No 40 Sheep Street, is stated to have previously been in the tenure of William Sheryve (or Shrif or Shreve). Of William, nothing is known, save that in a muster roll of 1536, he is listed in Sheep Street as an archer. The house is still known as The Shrieve's House to this day. William Shrieve would undoubtedly have been in the army of Henry VIII.

William Shrieve's successor to the house, John Jefferies, was a Catholic gentleman and well respected in the town. Whilst he practised his faith openly under the reign of Queen Mary, this became dangerous under her sister Elizabeth's reign. Priest holes have been found within the building, so it can be assumed that John Jefferies continued his Catholic practices in secret.

John's wife Margaret Jefferies was the mother of William Rogers (from her first marriage), who went on to be the tavern keeper. William and Elizabeth Rogers were close friends with William Shakespeare and it is believed that the famous character of Sir John Falstaff is based on his friend who ran The Three Tuns Tavern. Elizabeth I is supposed to have been so annoyed that Shakespeare killed off Falstaff, that she demanded he write another play about him. Shakespeare wrote The Merry Wives of Windsor.

John Woolmer is the most well-known Stratfordian to have leased Shrieve's House, for it was he who negotiated the new Borough Charter with Charles II in 1664 and under it, ended his term as Bailiff as the first official Mayor of Stratford.

The lease passed to various tenants through the years, but by the 1940s was in such a wretched state, with leaking roof, bulging walls and much woodwork missing, that there was a real danger of its demolition, despite being scheduled as an Ancient Monument. Eventually, Anne Bannister, a dress designer who started an interior decoration business, took on the lease of the Shrieve's House in the 1980s and spent some £100,000 on its restoration. In 1987, the barn running parallel was demolished, to build a shopping precinct called the Shrieve's Walk.

Joan's daughter, Joanna, is now running a business with Anne Bannister's daughter, Jo, in London.

In 1998 Steve Devey took over the property for his antique and picture framing business. However, he soon realised that people were interested in visiting the inside and started to charge an entrance fee. From this the museum, depicting the house's long and varied history emerged.

Janet and John Ford took over in October 2007, who further developed and upgraded this popular museum in Stratford to relate the story of the Tudors. The only museum in the country to do so. The Shrieve's House is still occupied by the family, making it one of the oldest lived in houses in Stratford. The barn still houses the privately run museum, which can be visited by members of the public and which helps towards the upkeep and maintenance of this ancient building. The cobbled stone courtyard is the oldest in Stratford and it is still like walking back in time.

The first surviving lease on 40 Sheep Street, known as The Shrieve's House, dates from the 1540s. The rooms mentioned in an inventory from 1566 are: the Chamber over the Hall, three little Chambers, the Chamber 'over the entire', the Chamber of the 'parler' by the entry, the Brewhouse, the Boulting House, the Ewting house, the Fish house and unspecified sheds. There must also have been a parlour, a kitchen, probably a buttery and possibly other rooms. The entry, with its chamber above and carriageway to the street existed in some form by 1566, although there was no building on the adjoining plot. Shrieve's House was made of wattle and daub, in which a woven lattice of wooden strips called wattle is daubed with a sticky material usually made of some combination of wet soil, clay, sand, animal dung and straw.

The front range of the house as it now stands, was built all at one time and has never been substantially altered. There have been several fires at the Shrieve's House but it is the one in September 1595 that was most severe, as well as another fire which occurred on 9 July 1614. The main ground floor room contains timbers that are badly charred which could possibly date from one of the fires. During Tudor times, keeping the fires going (heat and warmth) was paramount, so that the fires were only dampened down at night. (Hence the name curfew or *coeur de feu*). Anyone allowing them to go out would be punished. (In Tudor times men could beat their wives with sticks no thicker than their thumbs, hence a further phrase, under your husband's thumb). This, together with the thatched roofs caused many fires.

Stratford banned thatched roofs on the houses within the boundaries of the town and in Elizabeth Rogers' case, also ordered people to build brick fireplaces.

159. The Plague

(Edited by John and Helen Hogg – Stratford Town Walk)

The Jefferies were probably the tenants of Shrieve's House at the time of the Bubonic Plague which came to Stratford in 1564 (the year of William Shakespeare's birth). The first reported victim was Oliver Gunne, who was apprenticed to Thomas Gethen, a tenant and weaver at the mercer's building (now the Garrick Inn at the top of Sheep Street). He died on 11th July that year, his death marked by a simple Latin phrase in the records: *Hic Incipit Pestis*, literally, 'here begins the plague'. Almost 100 years later, the Plague returned in 1643. The town was a little more prepared and organised plague wardens, who would pay infected families to keep themselves isolated in an attempt to restrict the spread of the disease. This failed to work and as a second measure, a plague 'village' was built nearby, and sufferers were sent there. Due to the poor living conditions at that time, the pestilence confined itself almost exclusively to the poorer areas of the town. A local myth concerns 'the Plague wall' at the Holy Trinity Church, where people, fearful of dying on unconsecrated ground, sat on the wall and poisoned themselves with the deadly nightshade that grew there, before toppling onto church property where they felt reassured that their souls would pass to heaven.

There is also the story of Charlotte Clopton, the daughter of Hugh Clopton, one time Mayor of London and local nobleman. Buried hastily after she contracted the disease, the family were distraught on visiting the tomb six days later, in order to bury her mother, who had also succumbed to the disease to discover that they had buried poor Charlotte alive! In the intervening period, she had dug her way out of the coffin and consumed a portion of her left arm before death finally took her.

160. Vellum (Wikipedia)

Vellum is a translucent material produced from the skin, often split, of a young animal. The skin is washed with water, then lime. Vellum is derived from the Latin word, Vitulinum, meaning 'made from calf', leading to old French, Vélin, (calf skin). The term often refers to a parchment made from calf skin, as opposed to that from other animals. Vellum is generally smooth and durable, depending on preparation and quality of the skin. The manufacture involves the cleaning, bleaching, stretching on a frame (a hearse) and scraping of the skin with a crescent shaped knife called a lunarium or lunellum. To create tension, scraping is alternated with wetting and drying. A final finish may be achieved by abrading the surface with pumice. It is then treated with a preparation of lime or chalk, to make it accept writing or printed ink.

The Government in 2016, decided not to dispense with this practice. There is another form of Vellum, which is made from vegetables, which is a quite different synthetic material, used for a variety of purposes, including plans, technical drawings and blue prints.

The next High Steward of Stratford is shortly to be inaugurated and this office will be commemorated on vellum.

161. Marie Corelli *(See also Cameo 55)*

Marie Corelli's grave is in Evesham Road Cemetery, just to the left, as you go in. Sadly, two to three years ago, her grave was vandalised. On the evening of Saturday 8th December 2013, the angel that has stood watch over Marie Corelli's grave was pushed to the ground and smashed. The angel, slightly less than life size, was left face down in the turf with its right arm in pieces, and its left wing broken. At the time, it was thought to be irreparable. It is made of the most wonderful white marble and the broken pieces have been kept very safely ever since. Nicholas Birch, who is a director of Avon

Marie Corelli's grave.

Boating, is a lover of Marie Corelli. He has taken it under his wing, to have Marie Corelli's stone repaired. At no cost to the public, apart from the transportation to London, it will be cared for by the students of the Royal College of Art. Once repaired, which will be the only other cost, it will be transported back to Evesham Road Cemetery and put back in its proper place.

162. Town Boundaries

Town boundaries have been mentioned before, because they have been, over the centuries, in a state of flux. Yet again, in 2015, they were changed. The new boundary names are: Bishopton, Avenue, Clopton, Welcombe, Tiddington, Bridgetown, Guild Hall, Shottery and Hathaway. The old boundary of Old Stratford and Drayton has been engulfed in the new wards to the north west.

163. Harvard House *(See also Cameo 73)*

As this book progresses, extra information comes to light. Harvard University, through a British trust, administered the property until 1990, when the Shakespeare Birthplace Trust assumed responsibility for it. From 1996 to 2010, it was the Museum of British Pewter, following the generous donation to the Shakespeare Birthplace Trust of the Neish Pewter Collection and the fitting out of Harvard House to accommodate it. The Neish Pewter Collection now resides at Stirling Museum. (The future of Harvard House is still under debate).

164. The English Civil War

The English Civil War was a series of armed conflicts and

political machinations. Between the Parliamentarians (Roundheads) and the Royalists (Cavaliers) in the kingdom of England, over principally, the manner of its government. The first (1642–1646) and the second (1648–1649) wars pitted the supporters of King Charles I against the supporters of the Long Parliament, while the third (1649–1651) saw fighting between supporters of King Charles II and supporters of the Rump Parliament. The war ended with the Parliamentarian victory at the Battle of Worcester. Hostilities took place between 22nd August 1642 and 3rd September 1651. The wars lasted nine years, one week and five days. A part of these skirmishes was played out close to Stratford at the battle of Edgehill.

The overall outcome of the wars was threefold. The trial and execution of Charles I, the exile of his son Charles II and the replacement of the English monarchy with, at first, the commonwealth of England. Constitutionally, the wars established the precedent that an English monarch cannot govern without Parliament's consent. Although the idea of Parliament as the ruling power of England, was legally established as part of the glorious revolution in 1688. During the war, as has been mentioned in the section on Stratford Town Hall, the undercroft of the Town Hall was used to store gunpowder. The first fire in Stratford Town Hall was caused by this gunpowder exploding. Stratford Town Hall was built in the reign of Charles I and throughout its chequered history, has seen calamitous events, including this gunpowder explosion in 1643. The explosion destroyed, apart from most of the Town Hall's Shakespeare's hall, a valuable painting by Gainsborough of David Garrick.

165. The Domesday Book *(See also Cameo 35)*

The Domesday Book, or Books, because there are two, led to the formation of the Land Registry.

There are two independent works, one the Little Domesday Book and two, the Great Domesday Book. These can be viewed online.

166. The Guillotine

The guillotine was invented by Dr Joseph Guillotin. It was first used in France in April 1792, to end life without inflicting pain. It was last used in 1977.

167. The Guild Hall

On 2nd March 2016, in the afternoon, the doors of the Guild Hall, in which the first Borough Council held their meetings, will be opened for the public to view the inside of this restored building, following a major refit and with the aid of several grants. It has been returned to pristine glory. (More later)

Hoarding advertising the major restoration of the Guildhall.

168. Pubs Galore
A sample of the many, many pubs that were listed in Stratford's archives. (This will be researched in depth in the next Volume).

169. New Place
This is a project for the anniversary year of 2016 which is not yet complete. A photograph will be added in the next Volume showing it in its entirety and text will be added.

170. Tim Peake
Major Tim Peake, Britain's newest astronaut, is still in orbit as I write this and in my next Volume, this story will be updated.

171. Richard the Lionheart *(See also Cameo 14)*
Richard was the elder brother of John I, notorious because of the Magna Carta. John succeeded Richard I

Hoarding surrounding New Place at the beginning of its restoration.

Time Peake (left) celebrating 100 days in space.

after Richard's death. John I's coronation was in 1199. He fainted during the ceremony. Whenever John travelled on a ship or other modes of transport, two servants held his head for the whole journey. John travelled to the Holy Land to fight in the Crusades, as his brother did. Saladin, the leader of Jerusalem, blocked all the wells to cause dehydration. In 1199, Richard killed John to become King and in 1209, Genghis Kahn invaded China and Ninxia. Plantagenet King John sold charters to make money in 1215, John having been accused of abusing his power. It was a battle between the barons and King John. The barons agreed to barter the Magna Carta which was sealed by King John. It was a law for everyone, including the sovereign, but the trouble was, King John chose to ignore it. It was the foundation of democracy, 800 years old last year. King John died in 1216. When his son became king, he ignored the Magna

Carta but it became the foundation of the constitution of America, indicating that America chose to copy it.

Dover Castle, a medieval castle in Kent, was the jewel in the Plantagenet crown and was founded in the 11th Century. It has been described as the key to England, due to its defensive significance throughout history. It is the largest castle in England.

Joan McFarlane as a Town Councillor in 2015 cadging a lift on her way back from the Birthday Celebrations.

VOLUME 6

It is Thursday 8th September 2016 and Jayne and I are launching into Volume 6 of my book of Historic Cameos. Our book can be a little disjointed because I only write about things placed in front of me. This volume is going to be all about history in the making (at least the first part of it)

Much money for the following is being drawn from trust funds, and both private and public grants. The list of buildings I would like to talk about will include: New Place, The Guild Chapel, The Guildhall, Bell Court, The New Hospital, Hotel du Vin, and Fordham House.

There are big plans afoot for the refurbishment of Stratford-upon-Avon station. All of these will be completed by the end of 2017 with the exception of New Place which has already opened.

* * * * *

172. New Place (The Observer)
New place opened to the public after a six million pound refurbishment on Saturday 20th August 2016 at 11.00 a.m. The Cameos will not necessarily be in any order, so we will start with New Place.

The new oak and bronze gateway is the starting point for visitors to walk in the playwright's footsteps and meet the man behind the most famous works ever written. New Place is where Shakespeare had his family living with him for 19 years and where he died 400 years ago. Heavy rain in June delayed the opening.

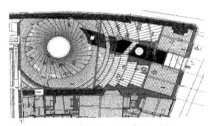

This plan shows the footprint of the building picked out in bronze on the ground. It shows the front gatehouse, the side service range, the inner courtyard with the well, and at the back, the domestic quarters, where Shakespeare lived and worked with his family.

Visitors will be welcomed across the original threshold through a splendid door of English oak and bronze.

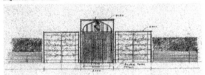

The family home, arguably the most special part of the site, is defined by a deep contemplation pool, with a light shining brightly from beneath the still water. The pool is surrounded by a seating and a circle of planting. The influence of Shakespeare's work is illustrated by the ripples spreading into the gardens.

Art pieces, such as Shakespeare's chair, the tempest galleon and a five gabled building, which is possibly what the gatehouse looked like, will be placed along the linear garden and in the courtyard as a reminder of times past.

Where we can, we will show the archaeology that we've discovered and incorporate them into the design.

None of the fine detail has been settled on yet, but we can show you the direction in which we are taking. We would love to hear your views, so please download a feedback form to fill in and return to us at the following address:

New Place Project
Shakespeare Birthplace Trust
Henley Street
Stratford-upon-Avon
CV37 6QW

Sketch of New Place before the restoration was started.

The setback was a bonus for the team, as during the excavation of the site, Nash's House next door was extended, which belonged to Thomas Nash. The original plans behind the new exhibition in this house had to be rethought. The excavation uncovered the Bard's kitchen. The refurbishment of New Place was the biggest project of its type in the world, to mark the anniversary of Shakespeare's death.

Shakespeare was 32 when he bought New Place in 1597, he remained there until he died in 1616. It was the largest house in the borough with 10 fireplaces, 20 rooms and extensive gardens.

The only remaining pillar from the ground floor of the town hall.

The last house to occupy this plot was demolished by the infamous Reverend Francis Gastrell in 1759 and the largest part of Shakespeare's estate has been preserved as a garden ever since. Shakespeare's lost house has been outlined in grave bronze inlaid into the stone paving, with a swathe of golden plants in a bronze clad raised border which enfolds his original well.

In the garden, as the photograph shows, one of the columns which supported the upper floors of the Town Hall, is for all to see. The ground floor of the Town Hall at that time, was an open market.

173. The Guild Chapel

The Guild Chapel dates back a thousand years, although it was not a chapel to begin with. This famous part of the Historic Spine of Stratford-upon-Avon, is on the opposite corner to New Place. The Guild Chapel is now looked after by Stratford Town Trust and this year received a £100,000 grant from the Heritage Lottery Fund. Now, for the first time volunteer guides are in the chapel to help visitors and one hundred visitors or more, visit every day and see it for themselves.

The walls inside were covered extensively with medieval wall paintings, many of which have been under lock and key for a very long time. The most famous wall painting is The Doom which is over the chancel arch. I will probably denote a Cameo to that a little later. The Allegory on Death, or Death Poem, found on the west wall within the chapel has for decades been covered by wooden panelling to protect it, as have several others.

The painting illustrates the transitory nature of earthly glories and the suffering for sins following death, a subject which was popular in the medieval times when it was painted. It was one of the best preserved wall paintings found within the Chapel which houses some of the finest medieval frescos in the whole of Europe. The Guild Chapel wall paintings were uncovered in the 19th and 20th centuries, having been lime washed on orders given to John Shakespeare through the borough council by King Henry VIII as part of the reformation.

As an aside, on 6th September 1586, the aforementioned John Shakespeare, William's father, lost his seat as an alderman due to his non-attendance at council meetings in the Guild Hall.

Another aside, because of the dissolution of the monasteries when King Henry VIII wanted to marry again, when he was married to Catherine of Aragon, the lady who caught his eye was Anne Boleyn, her lady in waiting. Already pregnant, King Henry VIII and Anne married in secret in 1553. He passed the Act of Supremacy, declaring that he was Head of the English Church and appointed Thomas Cranmer as Archbishop of Canterbury, who annulled Henry's marriage to Catherine.

There is a stained glass window in the Guild Chapel to commemorate President Kennedy.

174. The New Bell Court (Stratford Herald)

The new Bell Court is starting to take shape which includes a state of the art multi-screen cinema. The old building was demolished on 16 February 2016.

The steel frames that will form the structure of the cinema are currently being put into place. The cinema will be operated by the Everyman chain when it opens. In addition to the cinema which will be on the first floor of the building, three ground floor units will be built as well as a larger unit adjacent to the cinema. This 30 million pound development is due for completion early in 2017.

As the name implies the original curfew bell will be reinstated. At the moment, it is being cared for at Taylor's Bell Foundry in Loughborough and we are waiting to welcome it home, where it will be a feature in the aforementioned Bell Court.

175. The New Hospital (Stratford Herald)

Plans for this multi-million pound hospital received planning permission in October 2014. There will be a new eye unit, made up of an outpatients' suite and a special cancer unit. Building work started in December 2015 and the hospital is due to be finished early in 2017.

A computer generated preview of the new Stratford Hospital.
(Opening due July 2017).

The hospital will hopefully become a centre of excellence for cancer treatment and eye treatment. The million pound target for donations towards this brand new hospital made front page news in the Stratford Herald at the end of February 2017.

176. Stratford Railway Station

Plans have been on the cards for Stratford Railway Station for some time. The £500,000 project to fund new facilities, such as a new café, waiting room and retail area were first announced in June 2015 and when it actually happens I will be one of the first to know.

177. The Ferry Inn, Alveston (Stratford Herald)

The Ferry Inn held its 150th anniversary as a fully licensed public house at the end of 2016.

A public house has stood on this land which was owned by the Hirons family, who had farmed in the village since 1658.

In 1772 the Alveston Enclosure Act came into force and the land was consolidated into larger holdings, with the Hirons being allocated 274 acres. Records suggest it became less and less useful to the family and the land and buildings were sold several times before the farmhouse became what was then known as a beer house.

In 1838 William Wincote became the publican. It remained in the Wincote family for several generations and in 1866 William's grandson, John, was granted a spirits licence which meant the beer house became a public house and was known as the Exchange Inn. It became the Ferry Inn in 1962.

178. Shakespeare's School Room and Guild Hall
   (Google)

The Guild Hall was originally called the Rood Hall, which was virtually the village hall, where the residents of Stratford met and had feasts, amongst other things. The town's ancient 15th century Guild Hall and William

The newly restored Guildhall in Church Street.

Inside the school showing the Pedagogue's Chair.

Shakespeare's school room have recently undergone a major restoration project at a cost of 1.4 million pounds, now open for the first time to the public as a heritage attraction, in the heart of the town.

The school room provides the missing chapter in the story of Shakespeare's earlier life, his education and his inspiration to act and write.

A visitor can experience the very room where Shakespeare was educated and inspired to become the world's greatest playwright. They can also learn about the extraordinary history of the ancient Guild Hall and its part in the civic history of the town.

It has over 600 years of involvement in the key social and religious aspects of the town, including Shakespeare's father John, who played a leading role on the council that met therein. Previous residents were the Guild of the Holy Cross, who moved there, having left the Guild Chapel, which was their initial meeting place.

The interactive experience includes soundscapes, projections, films and interpretative panels with actors on hand with many anecdotes, to bring Shakespeare's story and those of the Guild Hall to life. Built in 1420, the Guild Hall is one of only a dozen surviving examples of a late medieval, provincial Guild Hall. It is home to a series of extremely rare medieval wall paintings, showing the seal of the Guild of the Holy Cross.

During the restoration work, medieval paintings never ever seen before, were uncovered by the experts working on the restoration.

In 1456 Master Thomas Jolyffe was a priest of the Guild of the Holy Cross in Church Street. There is no evidence that he ever taught in a school but his mother and father gave money for the education of boys in Stratford. In 1482 he endowed the Guild School with property, the income from which enabled a schoolmaster priest to be employed in Stratford "to teach grammar freely to all scholars coming to the (Guild) school". In the Guild Chapel there is a picture of Thomas Jolyffe in a stained glass window.

179. Hotel du Vin

A new hotel is set to open its doors in the heart of Stratford-upon-Avon in 2017, after permission was given to transform two Georgian listed buildings. Stratford District Council approved an application by the Malmaison Hotel du Vin Group to convert the Rother Street properties into a new 48 bedroom hotel. The chain currently owns 17 hotels across the country. Two Georgian listed properties were purchased from Stratford Town Trust in 2015 and will be the second for the chain in the Midlands. The Grade II listed property will feature a meeting room, private dining rooms, a bistro and separate banqueting rooms.

Joan is of the opinion that this has been a hotel in a previous life and will check for a future cameo. Watch this space…

180. George Clifford & Sons Stone Masons
(Stratford Observer)

This family firm has been based in the same Sanctus Street in the heart of the old town for 125 years. It is still going strong, thanks to the fourth and fifth generation of Cliffords. Stuart is the current Clifford at the helm and his sons, Jake and Tom, are now working for the company, making mostly headstones, as they have been for the past century and a quarter, since the firm was founded by George Clifford Senior in 1891. A real character, is how he was described. He was a superb carver and in between carving letters, he would have a sip of beer or whiskey. George Junior, one of the founder's three sons, was also a character. He had a deep mistrust of hospitals and refused to allow his wife to be

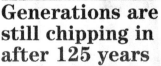

The Clifford Family of stonemasons (Evesham Road).

169

admitted for a gallstone operation. Instead, he got the surgeon to come to the stone masons yard and perform the operation there. It was successful and the removed stones still sit in a jar at the yard.

The firm quickly became a byword for quality and shortly after the end of the First World War, the company was approached by the War Graves Commission to provide headstones for those who had fallen on the battlefields of the Western Front.

Stuart and his Dad, Jack, visited the war graves of the Somme and Ypres, to see some of the tombstones that the firm had produced. They took with them, traced rubbings of some of the headstones, so that they knew what they were looking for. All of the war graves commissions were done to a rigid specification but Stuart says he can still tell the Clifford ones anyway. The firm is unusual in that it does not just carve stones, but makes them from scratch, cutting them from rocks sourced in Italy and closer to home in York. George Clifford & Sons is that all too rare example of a traditional firm which does things the traditional way and with real pride and passion.

181. John Shakespeare's Death (An Aside)

John Shakespeare, William's father was buried on 8th September 1601. *(See cameo 219).*

182. Fordham House

Fordham House was previously called Warwick House. It was not a beautiful building to look at, as it was built on stilts to accommodate the car park underneath. Warwick House was purchased from Stratford Town Trust in 2015. The company who now own it, Orbit Housing Association, took over lease of the building in 2016 but Stratford Town Trust have kept ownership of the freehold. The foundations for 82 apartments have been started. Orbit's original idea was to name the building Merchants' House, but Joan, who was on the Town Trust at the time, decided that because of its brewery connections and the fact that the Flower family had been such amazing benefactors to the town, it should be named after them. Orbit Housing Director, Adam Cooper, agreed with this suggestion and changed the name to Fordham House after Edward Fordham Flower, the brewer. The total cost of the build will be 10.4 million pounds and the topping out ceremony took place at the end of 2016.

Situated on a prime location on the corner of Birmingham Road and Clopton Road, it was the site of the Flower Brewery Cooperage, the Brewery itself

Edward Flower's wife, Celina.

being on the opposite corner. To mark the start of the construction of the new homes, Orbit and Stratford Town Trust were recently joined on site by partners, Deeley Construction and ABD Developments, to celebrate the laying of the first brick.

Because of Joan's suggestion on the change of name, she offered to research some old pictures of the brewery. She and Adam have spent many months delving into the archives at the Shakespeare Birthplace Trust and have send to Orbit's photography department, their chosen few. These will be displayed on the several landings of this very large building, including the foyer.

Due for completion in the summer of 2017 Fordham House will offer a mix of high quality one and two bedroom apartments for private rent. Magnetic walls will be installed for easy picture hanging, mobile parking bollards and mobile connected intercom system will be installed. With close proximity to the hospital and town centre, initial preference for the 82 apartments will be given to local key workers, such as health and emergency service workers and teachers, as well as local people.

183. Escheator

In medieval times, if someone died with no one to inherit their estate, the land would revert to The Manor in absence of legal heirs or claimants. The Escheator for the council in the early years, was the High Steward.

Leopards can be seen on the town coat of arms. People at the time, thought that a leopard was a hybrid between a lion and a panther. Joan has just thought of these to add because of their importance. Faces, which can be seen on the Mayor's chain of office, indicate a strong connection with the Kings of England.

184. Sir Hugh Clopton

Sir Hugh Clopton was a benefactor in many ways. His benefaction included the building of the stone Clopton Bridge, having been a wooden bridge before. Clopton Bridge had its 500th birthday during Joan's mayoralty in 1955.

His father's name was John and his mother's name was Agnes. Hugh as a young man, moved to London where he became Lord Mayor in 1491. He returned to Stratford-upon-Avon following his father's death and bought the Clopton estate.

185. Flower Family Tree

- Richard Flower Fordham
- His son – Edward Fordham Flower (born 1862) four times Mayor.
- His son – Charles Edward Flower (born 1879).
- His sons – Edgar and William. Edgar's son was Sir Arthur H Flower (born 1885).
- Archibald Flower (born 1915).
- His son was Fordham Flower.
- Fordham Flower's daughter was Elizabeth Flower.
- Elizabeth Flower's daughter, Léonie.

186. Movement of Sheep

In medieval times, sheep farmers drove their sheep across Stratford Bridge to sell them at market. Freemen of the town were excused the Bridge toll that had to be paid by other people. Shakespeare did not need any inspiration from Londoners and using the example of driving sheep across London Bridge, to write shepherds into his plays.

187. The Toll House

(Wrapped up for Christmas 2016)

Due to be reopened, following completion of refurbishment in June 2017.

This is additional information, researched by Joan in 2017:

- 1814 – The third floor was added.
- 1839 – The levy came to an end.
- 1840 – Tolls ceased on the bridge.
- 1841 – The house was rented for domestic use. In that year there were seven residents. Joan discovered in the 1841 Census: Elizabeth Bradley (aged 30, Toll House keeper), Mary Bradley (aged 35), Elizabeth Bradley (aged 1), Joseph Hewins (aged 20, agricultural labourer), Sarah Hewins (aged 25), Sarah Hewins (aged 7 months) and Joseph Masters (aged 15, Toll House keeper).

Interior view of the Toll House undergoing refurbishment

Old painting of Clopton Bridge viewed from the south.

- 1846 – Several chimneys were dismantled. There were many fireplaces – it must have been a very cold building for its tenants. At the same time it was turned into the office of James Cox timber business.
- 1951 – The toll house was listed Grade I.
- 1997 – James Cox's office closed for good.
- 2007 – The toll house was in the ownership of Stratford District Council and under the auspices of the Stratford Society, the only remaining chimney was removed and the building was made watertight. It is not known when the upper floor was removed.

Next door to the Toll House is Railway Cottage. The inhabitants were George Days, aged 50, agricultural labourer, Sarah Days, aged 45 and their children, Susannah Days, Thomas Days, George Days and John Days. Joan thinks that the Toll House and Railway Cottage were the beginnings of social housing.

188. King Edward VI School

Jayne Seymour died on 25th October 1537 after giving birth to Prince Edward, who later became King Edward VI and was instrumental in saving and supporting King Edward VI School as we know it today.

189. The Neighbourhood Plan

On 27th June 2011, the Neighbourhood Plan for the District began its gestation period. On 4th October 2016, the finished Plan was handed to Stratford Town Council, who has taken ownership of it. In 2017, there is to be a referendum by Stratford District Council which has to be won by a majority decision of the townspeople. If successful, 25% of the Community Infrastructure Levy will be received by Stratford Town Council.

1. The Neighbourhood Plan is a Plan for the town of Stratford-upon-Avon.

2. The Core Strategy is a Plan for Stratford District.

These two Plans have to coincide. The Core Strategy states that 3,500 houses excluding Tiddington and Alveston have to be in place by the year 2031. 2,400 of them are already built and 1,000 are still to be provided. Tiddington, by law, has to receive 113 houses and Alveston village, 32 houses. A very important brownfield site is where the canal traverses Stratford and is so important to the future of the town. This is going to be known as the Canal Quarter and is a prime site for development, which will bring much needed revenue to the town.

190. Hallowe'en

All Hallows' Evening or All Saints Evening is a three day observance of All Hallow Tide which is dedicated to the dead including all saints and martyrs and all the faithful departed.

191. Bell Court (Further news)

Walking through with difficulty, the refurbishment of Bell Court, I have made friends with a lot of the paviours. Following the question, "Do you ever get bored?", the answer was "No, suicidal". Because between us, we worked it out that they were laying 60,000 granite bricks! He told me that on several occasions, they have had to take them all up again to put in cables that another section had forgotten to install.

(Excerpt taken from Stratford Herald October 2016)

"Excitement surrounding Stratford's 30 million pound Bell Court development is building after two major restaurant chains confirmed they will be opening at the site. The Miller & Carter Steakhouse and bar

Bell Court under construction.

chain, All Bar One, will open at Bell Court early next year, joining burger restaurant Byron and Everyman cinemas in occupying units. John Stacey, Asset Management Director UK & European Investments said, "Construction of the new buildings at Bell Court is now nearing completion and refurbishment of the existing units is well underway, meaning we're on track for the development to open to the public in the spring (2017)." The finished date for groundwork was 22nd February 2017. The contract is overrunning a little and a final walkaround by the developer, to make sure everything was in place, was on Monday 28th February 2017."

192. The Play's the Thing – The Swan Theatre
(Stratford Herald)

"The Play's the Thing, a new, permanent, family-friendly exhibition in its Stratford-upon-Avon headquarters, which promises to reveal the behind-the-scenes secrets and stories of nearly 140 years of Shakespeare performances in and around the building. The Victorian Gothic rooms of its Swan Wing are a hive of noisy, smelly activity, reverberating to the bangs of a nail gun, as startling as the knocks at Macbeth's gate at dawn…

This is the brainchild of Geraldine Collinge, the RSC's director of events and exhibitions. In addition to the interactive fun, the exhibition will feature some real heavyweight exhibits, including the Chandos portrait of the poet, the only picture thought to have been made of Shakespeare during his lifetime, on loan from the National Portrait Gallery and a first folio of the playwright's work."

193. Boarders At King Edward VI School

(King Edward VI School – Published in 2008)

The school's Enquiry Commission of 1867 stated that there were no boarders at King Edward VI School. It is clear that during the headship of Thomas Medwin from 1843, there had been a small number of boys who had boarded. Master West of Alscot Park had lived in the house of the Reverend Joseph Greene, when he was headmaster during the middle of the 18th century. There are no surviving records of any boarders at the school from that time until the years of Medwin.

As a result of the Schools Enquiry, a scheme was suggested saying that the school should, should they wish, have boarders. The Governors agreed and in 1877, purchased a large house to provide an official residence for the headmaster. Opposite the lower entrance to New Place Gardens in Chapel Lane, the house had been the private school owned by a Mr Warrilow. It was then enlarged, with the view of accommodating boarders and had become known as School House. Before even one boy was welcomed, the headmaster encountered opposition. They presumably were charging a lower figure, a landlady in Old Town having placed a notice in the Stratford Herald advertising rooms for boys in her house. This was a serious challenge to the Governors' plans, but they could do little about it. They set up a visiting committee to ensure that the accommodation the lady offered was satisfactory.

In his history of the school, published in 1953, Lesley Watkins wrote that the idea of boarders was not quickly accepted and that a year after the Revered Laffan had arrived, admittedly a year of great trade depression in 1886, the school had no more than three official boarders.

The tide began to turn in its favour. The following year there were six, then 11 and in 1892, there were 20 boarders and six resident masters in School House. Laffan urged the outright purchase of The Old Vicarage to allow for the expansion of boarding. Thomas Pargetter, boarded from 1888, the first of three generations of boys to attend the school. His son was stroke in the first school four and his grandson won first 15 colours and played rugby for England.

At a full inspection by the Board of Education in 1929, there were 224 day boys and 43 boarders, having followed the recommendation of the 1925 inspection, particularly with the expansion of accommodation, which came at the time of serious economic decline in the country in 1934. The decline was noticeable because there were 218 boys and only 15 boarders. The Inspector stated that the vital question for the school was the question of numbers. It is an ancient school with an honourable history. The numbers at that time were so inadequate that the future was looked upon with serious misgiving. The Inspector stated that any change in the character would be most regrettable and the task of the Governors and the County Authority should take whatever steps they could to secure a larger entry.

The Inspectors identified the areas from which the boys were drawn. 55.5% from Stratford-upon-Avon, 26.9% from the rest of Warwickshire and 17.6% from the rest of England. These were from counties bordering Warwickshire or even further afield, principally southern England.

At the speech day and prize distribution held in July that year, Sir Charles Grant Robertson, Principal of Birmingham University, made reference to the report by the Inspectors "Look at your environment! Stratford is situated in the hub, the centre of the English speaking world. You have a river, you have an historic town which is the mecca for all who value what English poetry and English drama have done for this country and the world – an environment second to none. You've got all the setting that any educational home requires. Any boy going daily to school in Stratford through the historic streets, surrounded by ancient buildings with the spiritual wires in the electrical and moral ether, must take something away with him, apart from what he is going to learn from the teachers or to attain from examinations past.

The numbers continued to decline. Already by 1931, boarders had left The Old Vicarage and Trinity House was put up for sale. In 1933, Jolyffe House was closed. When Mrs Knight, the headmaster's wife died in 1936, the closure of School House was inevitable and in 1938 boarding finally ended. Leslie Watkins later wrote, "By the next term, had come the international scare, which resulted in the panic movement of the children from cities again and within another year the war had brought the mass evacuation to the country. All the boarding accommodation at the school could have been filled over and over again, but the door had been closed, the key turned in the lock and it was too late."

194. New Place (New Place Exhibition)
William Shakespeare bought New Place in 1597. It was the only home he ever purchased for himself and his family – his wife Anne and their daughters Susannah and Judith. Shakespeare's son, Hamlet, died aged 11 in 1596, the year before the house was purchased.

It is thought that Shakespeare paid about £120 for New Place. At the time, yearly income of a Stratford schoolmaster was about £20.

New Place was the largest house in the centre of Stratford, located next to the Guild Chapel, it was an impressive property, appropriate to Shakespeare's wealth and social standing.

Shakespeare owned New Place for 19 years until his death in 1616. During this time, he wrote more than half his plays. The house itself, was built in 1483 by Hugh Clopton. In 1540, New Place is described as a pretty house of brick and timber. New Place is recorded as having ten fireplaces.

View of the Knot Garden of New Place.

In 1602 Shakespeare bought 107 acres of land in Stratford for £320. In 1605, Shakespeare paid £440 for a share in the Stratford tithes, an annual tax from which he made about £60 a year.

195. Shakespeare's Stratford

Stratford-upon-Avon is where William Shakespeare was born, educated, lived his early adult life, married and became a father.

It is also in Stratford that Shakespeare makes his substantial financial investments. These included his purchase of New Place, the other houses that he let and the farmland from which he received rental income.

William's father, John Shakespeare, was awarded a coat of arms in 1596. This meant that following his father's death, Shakespeare could call himself a gentleman. At the time, Stratford had a population of about 2,500 people but there were only 45 gentlemen. Some had been born into the title, while others were businessmen who successfully applied for their own coat of arms.

Four gentlemen in Stratford are known to have carried a sword as a symbol of their status. Shakespeare may well have been one of these, as in his Will, he leaves his sword, an important and intimate possession, to a close friend.

The Mayor of Stratford-upon-Avon also carries a sword in procession, as an indication of their status.

196. Timeline of Shakespeare's Plays

(Royal Shakespeare Theatre Website)

We don't know exactly when Shakespeare started writing plays, but they were probably being performed in London by 1592. It is believed that he wrote around

38 plays, including collaborations with other writers. Shakespeare is likely to have written his final plays just a couple of years before his death in 1616.

1580-1590

The Taming of the Shrew – Considered to be one of Shakespeare's earliest works, the play is generally believed to have been written before 1592.

1590-1600

Henry VI Part II – Believed to have been written in 1591 and Shakespeare's first play based on English history.

Henry VI Part III – Written immediately after Part II, a short version of the play was published in Octavo form in 1595.

The Two Gentlemen of Verona – Known to be written around the 1590s as it was mentioned by Francis Meres in his list of Shakespeare's plays in 1598, no firm evidence for a particular year

Titus Andronicus – Written in 1591/92, with its first performance possibly in January 1594.

Henry VI Part I – Generally assumed to be the *Henry VI* performed at the Rose Theatre in 1592.

Richard III – Could have been written in 1592, shortly before the plague struck, or in 1594 when the theatres reopened post-plague.

The Comedy of Errors – Was possibly written for Gray's Inn Christmas festivities for the legal profession in December 1594.

Love's Labour's Lost – An 1598 edition refers to it being 'presented before her Highness [Queen Elizabeth] this last Christmas', and most scholars date it to 1595-96.

A Midsummer Night's Dream – Often dated to 1595-96. Reference in Act 1 Scene 2 to courtiers being afraid of a stage lion may allude to an incident in Scotland in 1594.

Romeo and Juliet – Astrological allusions and earthquake reference may suggest composition in 1595-96.

Richard II – Typically dated 1595-96. Described in 1601 as 'old and long out of use'.

King John – Written between 1595 and 1597; an anonymous two-part *King John* was published in 1591 but Shakespeare's version is stylistically close to later histories.

The Merchant of Venice – Registered for publication in 1598, reference to a ship Andrew suggests late 1596 or early 1597 as a Spanish ship of the name was captured around that time.

Henry IV Part I – Probably written and first performed 1596-97, registered for publication in 1598.

Henry IV Part II – Written around 1597-98 and registered for publication in 1600, both parts are based on Holinshed's *Chronicles*.

Much Ado About Nothing – Late 1598, not mentioned in Francis Meres's 1598 list of Shakespeare's plays but included the role Dogberry for Will Kemp, a comic actor who left the company in early 1599.

Henry V – Written in 1599, mentions a 'general... from Ireland coming', could be referring to the Earl of Essex's Irish expedition in 1599.

As You Like It – Typically dated late 1599. Not mentioned in Francis Meres's 1598 list of Shakespeare's plays, unless originally called *Love's Labours Won*.

Julius Caesar – 1599. Not mentioned in Meres's

1598 list of plays, seen at the Globe by Swiss visitor Thomas Platter in 1599.

1600-1610

Hamlet – Dated around 1600, registered for publication in summer 1602. There are allusions to *Julius Caesar*, which was written in 1599.

The Merry Wives of Windsor – Estimated 1597-1601, though an allusion to the Order of the Garter may indicate that it was performed at the Garter Feast in 1597.

Twelfth Night – 1601. Not mentioned in Meres's 1598 list of plays and alludes to a map first published in 1599.

Troilus and Cressida – Dated 1601-02, registered for publication early 1603 and alludes to the play *Thomas Lord Cromwell*, which was registered for publication in 1602.

Othello – Dated 1604 though some argue for a slightly earlier date. It is recorded to have been performed in court in November 1604.

Measure for Measure – Performed at court for Christmas 1604, probably written earlier the same year.

All's Well That Ends Well – No strong evidence for date written or first performed, but it is usually dated 1603-06 on stylistic grounds.

Timon of Athens – Estimated 1604-06 based on stylistic similarity to *King Lear*.

King Lear – Dated 1605-06. Performed at court December 1606 and seems to refer to eclipses of September and October 1605.

Macbeth – 1606. Certainly more Jacobean than Elizabethan based on the play's severe compliments to King James.

Antony and Cleopatra – Dated 1606-07, registered for publication in 1608 and perhaps performed at court in 1606 or 1607.

Coriolanus – Perhaps written in 1608. Allusion to 'coal of fire upon ice' in Act 1 could refer to the great frost of winter in 1607/08.

Pericles – 1608. Registered for publication in 1608; Wilkin's novel *The Painful Adventures of Pericles*, cashing in on the success of the play, was published in 1608.

Cymbeline – 1610. A performance in 1611 is recorded. Theatres were reopened in spring 1610 after a long closure due to the plague.

AFTER 1610

The Winter's Tale – 1611. Performed at the Globe in May 1611; dance of satyrs apparently borrows from a court entertainment of January 1611.

The Tempest – 1611. Performed at court in November 1611; uses source material not available before autumn 1610.

Henry VIII – 1613. The first Globe theatre burnt down in a fire that started during a performance of the play on 29th June 1613.

The Two Noble Kinsmen – 1613-14; 'our loss' in the Prologue probably refers to the Globe fire of 1613.

197. Occupations of the Residents
(New Place Exhibition)

Stratford-upon-Avon was a busy market town. Between 1570 and 1630, there were 69 different occupations listed. These included:

24 tailors

23 glovers (including Shakespeare's father, John)

23 butchers
20 weavers
16 shoemakers
15 bakers
15 carpenters
12 blacksmiths
7 skinners
7 fullers (who cleaned wool before it was spun)
7 tanners (who made leather from animal skins)

198. Restoration of the Guild Hall

When Joan visited the Guild Hall, prior to it being opened to the public, an unexpected discovery was made. On cleaning the wall at the end of the Guild Hall, an image was uncovered that had never been seen before, of St John the Evangelist. It is possible to see it now because having been restored, it is covered by a glass screen.

199. The Tomb of the Unknown Warrior

In 1916 the Reverend David Railton, a chaplain at the Front, noticed a grave in the garden in Armentieres with a rough cross bearing the words, "An unknown British soldier". After the war in 1920 he suggested that Britain honour its own unknown war dead officially.

Confirmed accounts say that four bodies were exhumed from four battle areas, the Aisne, the Somme, Arras and Ypres. The remains were covered with union flags and brought to the chapel of St Pol. Brigadier General L J Wyatt, who was the commander of British Forces in France and Flanders, then selected one. The officers placed the body in a plain coffin made from oak of Hampton Court and it was transported to Dover on the Destroyer HMS Verdun.

On the morning of 11th November 1920, the unknown warrior was drawn through crowd lined streets in a gun carriage in a procession to the Cenotaph where King George V placed a wreath on the coffin. At 11 o'clock the nation observed the Two Minutes Silence, after which the body was taken to Westminster Abbey and buried. The grave contains soil from France and is covered by a slab of black Belgian marble, inscribed with these words from the Bible, "They buried him among the kings because he had done good toward God and toward his house" 2 Chronicles, Chapter 24, Verse 16.

On Friday 11th November 2016, Joan once again attended once again, the Remembrance Day Service in Holy Trinity Church together with the Mayor and Town Council.

200. The Curfew Bell

(Joan and Juliet Short, the current Mayor of Stratford)

This very old bell was founded by Richard De Wymbis circa 1330. It has the inscription Criste. AVDI.NOS. It is 31¼ inches in diameter and strikes the note C. These markings are also found on bells in Westminster Abbey and this was among a small group of bells cast in London about 1320 to 1330 by Richard De Wymbis or his successor. It was therefore used as a church bell. How did it arrive in Stratford? Nobody seems to know. It used to be housed in the old timber framed Market Cross at the top of Bridge Street where it was used as a clock bell. When Market Hall was rebuilt on the present Barclays Bank site in 1821, the builder recycled the old weather vane, ironwork and the bell. It was hung in a domed octagonal turret and added to it, was a new striking clock by Warwick's Alexander Simmonds in 1816.

In 1909, Market Hall was converted into a bank where the clock and bell remained until 1959. To celebrate the new bank, Barclays asked John Smith & Sons of Derby to install a new striking clock, so the bell was put into the Corporation store in Guild Street where it remained until 1975 when it was used as part of an ornamental feature in the previous Bell Court shopping precinct. There was a plate on the brickwork, telling the history of the bell.

It was repositioned in 1991 under the roof of the entrance to the arcade in the renamed Town Square. It was taken down in 2015 and sent for repair to Loughborough where it has been in the safekeeping of Taylors, but never forgotten. It will return home soon in 2017.

The current Mayor, Juliet Short, (2016-2017) tells me that Val Harris and many at Stratford District Council saved it from a skip when they saw it being unceremoniously removed from Town Square. If it had not been saved, we would have lost something valuable and important to the town's history.

At five in the morning in the middle of February 2017, the infamous bell which has been in Stratford for centuries, returned to its home town, greeted by the mayor and site manager of what is now to be called Bell Court once again. The bell has been extensively restored in the bell foundry of Taylors of Loughborough, who have been looking after it since it hung in the previous Bell Court.

201. Siblings (Literary Genius)

Joan Shakespeare (1558-1558) – Joan was the first born of John and Mary Shakespeare who had eight children between 1558 and 1580. Joan died at the age of just two months old – the cause of death was believed to be the Bubonic Plague.

Margaret Shakespeare (1562-1563) – Margaret only lived for one year. The cause of death has not been documented but was believed to be due to the Bubonic Plague.

William Shakespeare (1564-1616) – William was the first born son of John and Mary Shakespeare and thankfully survived childhood unlike the two sisters before him.

Gilbert Shakespeare (1562-1612) – Two years after William's birth the Shakespeare's fourth child, Gilbert, was born. It is possible that he was named after Gilbert Bradley, a Burgess of Stratford who was also a glover as was John Shakespeare and lived in Henley Street. It is likely that Gilbert attended school with William. Gilbert took the trade of a haberdasher and followed his brother William to live in London. Gilbert often returned to Stratford and he appeared in Stratford court in connection with a lawsuit. Gilbert never married and remained a bachelor until his death in Stratford, on 3rd February 1612, at the age of 46.

Joan Shakespeare (1569-1646) – Joan was the fifth child of John and Mary Shakespeare and named after her deceased sister which was a common practice during the Elizabethan era. It was not the usual custom for girls in this era to attend school, so Joan would have stayed at home and helped her mother with the household chores. Joan met and married a hatter called William Hart. She had four children but only William and Michael survived. Joan's son, William Hart (1600-1639), followed his Uncle William's footsteps and became an actor. He never married but he is believed to have fathered an illegitimate son called Charles Hart who became a leading actor during the Restoration period. William gave permission for Joan to live in the western of the two houses on Henley Street where she stayed until her death at the remarkable age of 77 years old!

Anne Shakespeare (1571-1579) – Anne was born in 1571 when William was seven years old. She died when she was just eight years old – the cause is uncertain but it is probable that Anne died of the Bubonic Plague. Anne Shakespeare was provided with an expensive funeral even though the family were going through a financial crisis. She was buried on 4th April 1579.

Richard Shakespeare (1574-1613) – Richard was baptised on 11th March 1574. When Richard was born, the Shakespeare family fortunes were in decline and it is probable that Richard did not receive an education or read or write. There is little known about Richard. There are no records of a marriage but it is believed that he lived out his life in Stratford-upon-Avon helping with the family business. He was buried on 4th February 1613 – he lived to the age of 39.

Edmund Shakespeare (1581-1607) – At the time of the birth, the Shakespeare fortunes had recovered. Edmund was 16 years younger than William. He followed William to London and worked as an actor. Edmund died in 1607 at the age of 27 and once again it is believed that the cause was the Bubonic Plague. Edmund was buried in St Saviour's Church in Southwark in London on 31st December 1607. William paid for his expensive funeral which was attended by many of the Globe actors.

202. The Funeral of Jayne Seymour

Jayne Seymour was the third wife of Henry VIII and

mother of Edward VI. I have put this in because he rescued Edward VI Grammar School through the grant of a Charter. The funeral took place on 12th November 1537.

203. William Shakespeare's Time In London
(Stratford Observer)

Shakespeare did not go to London to pursue his love of the theatre; he went to work for the family's illegal wool business. These are the thoughts of David Fallow, financier, who has spent years studying Shakespeare's family's wealth and believes their riches to rags tale is not true. Historians say Shakespeare was a glover, a dealer in hides and wool, who went from a booming trade to bust, resulting in his son having to make his own wealth in the London theatre. Mr Fallow believes that instead of bankruptcy, the glover was reinvesting in wool and making more money than ever, some of it through shady deals.

It was the wool trade which prompted William to leave Stratford for London in 1585, so he could work as the family's business representative. For seven years, from 1585, are among Shakespeare's so called lost years, when academics know little of what the Bard was up to.

Financial records of the time and Stratford Court documents from John Shakespeare's illegal wool trading has led Mr Fallow to conclude the Shakespeares were never in poverty. He believes other historians have overlooked the information because they are qualified in literary studies and not in maths. You get some very brilliant academic writing about Shakespeare, he says, but the minute they try to talk about money or numbers, it becomes almost incomprehensible. John Shakespeare was a national level wool dealer and legal research coupled with analysis of the wool market, proves this. The Shakespeare family never fell into poverty.

When Shakespeare returned to London, he was able to afford shares in the Lord Chamberlain's Men, the theatrical company with whom he worked. Remarkably, there were large purchases of land in the Stratford area, including a house with up to 30 rooms and grounds requiring servants. The assumption has always been he became hard up, but Fallow's research builds a considerable argument on the idea that his fortunes did not decline, as has regularly been assumed, but because he had an alternative way of earning money, which was a bit shady.

Watch this space...

204. Mulberry Casket (Stratford Herald)

A beautiful casket believed to be carved from the original mulberry tree which Shakespeare planted when he lived at New Place was sold for £5,000 on 12 July 2016 in Sotheby's in London. John Marshall's shop was No. 21 Chapel Street, where he was a carver, upholsterer and house decorator. In 1756, the then owner, the Reverend Francis Gastrell, became tired of visitors to New Place and proceeded to attack and destroy the mulberry tree in the garden. Later Gastrell applied for permission to extend the garden. His application was rejected and his tax increased, so Gastrell retaliated by demolishing the house in 1759. This greatly outraged the inhabitants of Stratford and Gastrell was forced to leave town.

Believed to be created in 1860, local carver of the time, John Marshall, took the mulberry wood and created various caskets and chalices to sell on. On the back of the box is carved the words, Shakespeare's/ Mulberry Wood/J Marshall Carver/Stratford-upon-Avon, surrounded by the coat of arms of Shakespeare and his father. The other three sides have branches and leaves carved intricately across them.

On the top of the box is carved "Give me the key for this and instantly unlock my fortunes here", a quote from Aragon's speech in the Merchant of Venice. The green lined velvet bottom and purple velvet lined sided box contained a letter from the previous owner which Camilla Smith, the current owner, received along with the box. The two sided letter which Camilla received, explains the history of the box and New Place where the mulberry tree was cut down.

205. The Markets of Stratford

There were five markets in Stratford. One was located at Market Cross which was two storeys high, mentioned in previous Cameos and stood between what is now a jewellery shop called Fraser Hart which opened in 2016 and Barclays Bank. At this market, you could buy butter and cheese. The second was called Rother Market, which was a market for cattle and hides. The third was a pig market in Swine Street, in what is now known as Ely Street. The fourth was a sheep market in Sheep Street, which goes without saying. There were no crosses at any of these markets. The fifth was called Corn Market on the corner of Sheep Street and High Street.

206. Fraser Hart (Wikipedia)

William Hart was a Jacobean actor and the nephew of William Shakespeare. He was born in Warwickshire in

1600 and died probably in London in 1639. He was the son of Hatter, William Hart, and Shakespeare's sister Joan. He started as a child actor and eventually joined the famous troupe, the King's Men – his famous uncle's troupe, in the 1630s. He never married and is thought to have had an illegitimate child, called Charles who also became an actor.

It has been suggested that William Hart, who is mentioned in Shakespeare's Will, was the sole begetter, Mr WH, to whom the sonnets are dedicated. The sonnets are constantly for the begetter to marry and have children, and even refers to him bearing the looks of his mother. On the death of Shakespeare's own son, William Hart became Shakespeare's male heir and it is tantalising to think that the WH mystery has been solved. The only problem is, that when the sonnets were published, Hart was only nine years old. It is possible that the 1600 birth year is wrong, or that Shakespeare may have written the sonnets in anticipation of Hart's coming of age, and may have had to sell the sonnets to raise money quickly.

207. Joan Shakespeare
In 1569 John and Mary Shakespeare gave birth to another girl and named her after her firstborn sister, Joan. Joan Shakespeare accomplished the wondrous feat of living to be 77 years old – outliving William and all her siblings by decades. Joan married William Hart the Hatter and had four children but two of them died in childhood. Her son, William Hart (1600-1639) followed in his famous uncle's footsteps and became an actor, performing with the King's Men and in the mid 1630s, his most notable role was that of Falstaff. William Hart

never married, but the leading actor of the restoration period, Charles Hart, is believed to have been William Hart's illegitimate son and grandnephew of Shakespeare.

Due to the fact that Shakespeare's children and his other siblings did not carry on the line past the 17th century, the descendants of Joan Shakespeare and William Hart possessed the only genetic link to the great playwright. Joan Shakespeare lost her husband William a week before she lost her brother William in 1616, and she lived the rest of her life in Shakespeare's birthplace. Joan died in 1646 but her descendants stayed in Stratford until 1806.

208. The Rood Hall

In the beginning of the 15th century, the Guild Hall was originally built as the Gild's feast hall, together with the School House, known as Pedagogue's House (1427). It cost a little under £10 to complete. The timber cost 45 shillings and the source for these costings was "The Bill of Costs".

Latin was taught as it was required for University and the three professions; the law, medicine and the church, but also for those in business and those in local administration and for keeping records. The boys of King Edward VI school were only to speak in Latin.

The Headmaster was always an ordained minister until Leslie Watkins became Headmaster in 1945. In 1944 the Education Act required the School to decide whether it wished to be fully independent or part of the state system. It chose to be a voluntary aided school. As a result, all fees were abolished, boarders were no longer accepted and the preparatory school closed. Girls were accepted into the sixth form in September 2013.

The fraternity was bound by the rules of the Blessed Augustin but they were allowed special privileges such as clothing. Instead of pelisse, they were allowed to wear russet coloured wool and those in holy orders were to be clothed in an over tunic and a cloak. On the cloak's left shoulder was a cross of black fur, surmounted by a white mitre. The laity wore a cape with a similar cross and mitre on the left shoulder.

They had to sleep in a dormitory and eat in a refectory and were not allowed to wonder unduly around the town. The hospital found it had great influence and the Gild had rent charges poured into its coffers. As a result, it fell into loggerheads with the College. The Bishop of Worcester, Thomas, decreed that the Gild should pay proper tithes and oblations to the College.

It was customary in religious houses, to build the church on the north side to keep off the cold winds from the domestic apartments. On the south east, on the spot where the Old Vicarage stands, stood the dwelling for the chaplains of the Gild (now destroyed). At the south west corner, the old school stood with the chambers over it. On the north end, there was a porter's lodge and an entrance with depressed arches.

209. History of the High Steward

The first High Steward, as noted on the board in the Council Chamber, was in 1610. His name was George Baron Carew of Clopton and Earl of Totnes. He was appointed by the Chapter of King James I. Subsequently, in 1629, Sir Greville Verney KT, was elected. The other High Stewards can be noted by reading the list to the left of all the bailiffs and mayors of Stratford-upon-Avon, in the Council Chamber.

Originally, it was a judicial role with considerable powers but by the end of the 17th century, these powers had diminished into a largely ceremonial role. The Royal Charters of the 17th century stipulated that the High Steward should hold the rank of least a knight and also reserved to the Crown, the veto on the nomination.

Her Majesty Queen Elizabeth II happily agreed to the Marquess taking over the role, held from 1976 by Sir William Dugdale, until his death in 2014. The approbation warrant was signed by the Queen. As previously mentioned, the first High Steward in 1610 was George Baron Carew, 19 years later, Sir Greville Verney succeeded him. It is a job for life.

In 1532, Sir Thomas Lucy, a member of the Corporation, formed under the Charter of Incorporation in 1553 was often referred to as Steward. He was Shakespeare's cousin. He was often in London because he was also a member of Parliament. In his absence, the Common Clerk had to stand in for him.

Stratford has been granted many Charters. The Charter of 1610, King James I's Charter, tidied up some of the anomalies which had become apparent in the previous 50 years, adding a power of imprisonment or fine as a sanction for the non-observance of bylaws. It also extended the jurisdiction to include Old Town and adding two more fairs. More importantly however, it created the offices of High Steward, Recorder, Chamberlain and Common Clerk.

A further privilege conferred, was the right to have two maces, one bearing royal arms and the other the arms of the borough, which were to be carried before the mayor on ceremonial occasions. It appears that up until this time, the Corporation had been using civic regalia without any express authority. Both Charters ceased to be used in 1867.

Henry Jocelyn Seymour, 9th Marquis of Hertford, was appointed the 25th High Steward on Monday 29 February 2016.

210. Mary Ann Macleod (Mother of Donald Trump)

Mary MacLeod was born on the Isle of Lewis in Scotland. Her son, Donald, was made President of the United States on 20 January 2017.

211. The Swan Fountain

Christine Lee, Sculptor, designed and made the Swan Fountain in Joan's mayoral year, inaugurated by Her Majesty the Queen the following year. Jennifer Lee, author, and inspiration behind the hugely successful television series, Call the Midwife, was her sister.

212. The New Silk Road

The so called new Silk Road opened on 18 January 2017, when a large orange locomotive arrived in Barking Eurohub London, from Eastern China, in the city of Yiwu. The distance travelled was 7,500 miles and took from 3 January to 18 January 2017, to cross Europe, succeeding the infamous Silk Road at which Stratford-upon-Avon is situated at its end at Clopton Bridge.

All the dyes used in the medieval paintings in the Guild Chapel, must have been brought from Asia to Stratford along this route. Some of the colours are still very vivid.

The Maritime Silk Road is work in progress, with a new deep sea port on the Eastern Seaboard of China which is under construction.

213. King Henry VIII's Death

King Henry VIII died on 28 January 1547 at Whitehall Palace and his nine year old son became King Edward, rescuing the declining King Edward VI Grammar School for Boys in Stratford.

214. Swan-Hopping

(Researched and compiled by Roxanne Bennis)

In 1867 the Reverend G J Granville, upon retiring from Stratford to go to Pleasley Rectory in Derbyshire, presented his swans to the Stratford Corporation. This seems to have been an informal gift and circumstances soon led the Corporation to clarify their position.

The 19th century Borough Council's attitude towards the swans was similar to that of medieval lord, in that the swans were considered an asset and a status symbol, rather than ordinary wildlife. Swans could be purchased from the Corporation for the price of one guinea per cygnet, the first purchase being made by Mrs Starkey of Rhine Hill in 1868.

The Corporation also continued the more prosaic tradition of the swan as a delicacy for the table. Every year two cygnets were caught and prepared for the Mayor's Feast in September/October, where they appeared on the menu alongside tongues, pigeon pies, ducks and geese.

In order to maintain their exclusive right to the swans, it was necessary to mark them in some way, and the following year, in 1869, the Stratford Herald reported an "interesting ceremony" which, for almost the next 20 years was to be an annual fixture on the Council Calendar. Although the proper term for the procedure is "Swan-Upping", it was consistently referred to locally by the corrupted term "Swan-Hopping".

Every August or September, the swan-hopping party would assemble at Bridgefoot or the Unicorn dock and would consist of the Mayor, Borough Chamberlain, various Councillors, Macebearers, the Beadle, Superintendent of Police, Vicar of Holy Trinity Church, Headmaster of King Edward VI Grammar School, PC Harris (the town's semi-official swan-keeper) and other gentlemen and ladies of Stratford society. The party would row along the river, starting from Lucy's Mill as far up river as Tiddington, in search of swans. The swans would be corralled in a side creek or between the boats to be caught or driven up river in advance of the boats to be caught later. Procedures varied – they would be sometimes marked and released on the spot, or transported in boats up river to be marked in a meadow all at one time. This part of swan-hopping seems to have been a good two to three hours of "messing about in boats" and there are reports of a macebearer and a police officer falling in the river; mention of "a little splashing

Photograph of the Unicorn Hotel now called the Pen & Parchment.

and sprinkling, of which the ladies, by sheer accident, obtained rather more than their share" and a report of a worthy Alderman's beaver hat coming to grief by coming into contact with a weeping willow.

The method of marking the swans was to use a sharp steel punch to perforate a small hole in the web of the left foot. As this could heal over, it was necessary to catch all the birds each year to see if re-marking was needed. The perforating was done by Beadle one year and another time, the Mayor marked the first swan. The birds were also pinioned, to ensure their remaining in Stratford.

Afterwards, there was a picnic on the riverbank of bread, cheese and onion, with beer or whisky for the men and sherry for the ladies. This was followed by a leisurely row downstream to Stratford.

Although no definite numbers are given, there seems to have been 10 to 20 swans on the river at this time. Throughout the 1870s Stratford Corporation was very proud of its swans and swan-hopping, with newspaper articles referring to time-honoured customs and ancient ceremonies remaining as a local institution, and at pains to point out that the Stratford Corporation was one of only a few bodies with the privilege of marking their own birds. However, interest diminished gradually throughout the 1880s until by 1891 the old custom of swan-hopping was described as having fallen into disuse.

The ceremony was revived on 18 May 1996 for the 800th Anniversary celebrations.

215. Medieval Poem (from the Guild Chapel)
(One of the medieval poems uncovered by experts to the left of the clock tower, adjacent to the original door into Shakespeare's school)

This makes it so apparent how afraid people were
of death.
Earth upon Earth
Remember, man, that you are dust
And to dust you shall return.
Earth out of earth is wondrously wrought,
Earth has on earth a dignity of naught,
Earth upon earth has set all his thought
How that earth upon earth may be high brought.
Earth upon earth would be a king
But how earth to earth shall, thinks he not a thing;
When earth breeds earth and his rents home bring
Then shall earth of earth have full hard parting.
Earth upon earth wins castles and towers
Then says earth unto earth, "This is all ours!"
When earth upon earth has built up his bowers
Then shall earth for earth suffer sharp showers.
Earth goes upon earth as mould upon mould
He goes upon earth, glittering like gold,
As if earth never more return to earth should;
And yet shall earth unto earth go faster than he
would.
Now why that earth loves earth, wonder me think
Or why earth for earth should either sweat or
swink
For when earth upon earth is brought within
brink
Then shall earth of earth have a foul stink
Death dissolves all things.

(If you want to see the original poem in medieval English, please visit the Guild Chapel)

216. Osborne Court

Due to the lack of sewers and general sanitation, several courtyards in Stratford consisting of between eight and ten small cottages. Their waste was collected by the "midnight milkman" with a horse and cart. They were quite murky places to live in. Jayne and I have already mentioned one, called Emms Court in Sheep Street.

Walking through Bards Walk in Stratford today, 16 February 2017, I was reminded of this fact by looking up to a brass plaque on the wall which is situated above the door leading to Meer Street. It states: "This plaque marks the site of Osborne's Court, which comprised of eight cottages dating between 1809 and 1821. The cottages were converted from an old Malthouse by John Osborne and his son John, farmers and millers of Hampton Lucy and Charlecote, and were demolished in the late 1890s.

217. Chewers or Alleys

Ely Street takes its name from Eale Mill, a mill probably used for crushing seeds for oil. This was probably Ullemylle, which John Ulemaker was renting from the Gild, in 1407. There were several tenants of this mill and latterly, it became a Malthouse in 1599. In the middle of the 15th century, the mill in Swine Street, the old name for Ely Street, was in the possession of William Bole or Bull, Bailiff, 1444–1445 and afterwards by his widow.

218. Thought for the Day

The word typewriter is the only word that can be spelt using only the top line of a keyboard!

219. John Shakespeare (1531–1601) (Wikipedia)

Father of William Shakespeare. John Shakespeare was

the son of Richard Shakespeare of Snitterfield. He moved to Stratford-upon-Avon and married Mary Arden, with whom he had eight children, five of which survived into adulthood (see the end of this cameo for full details). He was a well to do glover and whittawer (a leatherworker) by trade. Shakespeare was a dealer in hides and wool and was elected to several municipal offices, serving as Alderman and culminating in a term as Bailiff. He was the Chief Magistrate of the Town Council before he fell on hard times, for reasons unknown to historians. His fortunes later revived after the success of his son and he was granted a coat of arms, five years before his death, probably at the instigation and expense of his playwright son. To be granted a coat of arms, meant that you could be a called a gent and being a gent had its advantages.

John Shakespeare moved to Stratford-upon-Avon in 1551, where he became a successful business man, involved in several related occupations. From 1556 to 1592, several official records identify him as a glovemaker, which was probably his primary trade. As tradition remembers him, following that trade even into his old age. But the records of his real estate purchases and legal expenses, indicate an income much higher than that of a small town tradesman. The administration of his father's estate in 1561, names him as a farmer. He inherited and leased agricultural land and is on record as selling timber and barley. Records also document him as a "brogger", an unlicensed and therefore illegal wool dealer. In addition, he bought and leased out houses. He was twice taken to court for violating the usury laws that prohibited charging interest higher than the legal limit of 10%.

By 1552, he was residing in a house in Henley Street. On 2 October 1556, he purchased a house on the same street, now known as the eastern wing of what is traditionally referred to as the birth place of William (now called Shakespeare's Birth Place). Whether it was the same house he was living in, in 1552, is unknown. In 1576, he bought two houses to the west and joined all three together.

In 1556, he was elected to the Borough as Ale Taster, the first of several key municipal positions he was to hold in Stratford. In that position, he was responsible for ensuring that weights and measures and prices were observed by innkeepers and publicans within the Borough. This also applied to butchers, bakers and town traders. In 1558, he was appointed Borough Constable – a position similar to an early police constable. In 1559, John became an Affeeror (correct spelling), an officer responsible for assessing fines for offences carrying penalties not explicitly defined by existing statutes. This role led to his becoming a Burgess, then a Chamberlain. He would have been known as a "goodman", a title that recognised his growing social status within Stratford. By 1564, John was an Alderman, a member of the Common Hall and it was in this year that William was born.

In 1568, John was appointed High Bailiff, the present day equivalent of Mayor, elected by the Common Council of Burgesses and Aldermen, which entitled him to be referred to as Master John Shakespeare. In that capacity he presided at the sessions of the Court of Record and at Council meetings. For his Borough, the Bailiff was Almoner, Coroner, Escheator and Clerk of the Market. He served as Justice of the Peace, in issuing warrants and negotiating with the Lord of the Manor on behalf of the Corporation.

In 1569, John had applied for his coat of arms, which after a long period of dormancy, was granted on 20 October 1596. Most historians believe that his son, William, reopened the application following his own literary and financial success in London.

John married Mary Arden, one of the Ardens of Warwickshire, a local gentry family and reportedly a niece of John Shakespeare's father, Richard Shakespeare. It is not known when they married, but a date around 1557 is assumed as there is a baptismal record for a "Joan Shakespeare, daughter of John Shakespeare" dated 15 September 1558. The Shakespeares had eight children: Joan (baptised 15 September 1558, died in infancy), Margaret (baptised 2 December 1562 – buried 30 April 1563), William (baptised 26 April 1564 – 23 April 1616), Gilbert (baptised 13 October 1566 – buried 2 February 1612), Joan (baptised 15 April 1569 – buried 4 November 1646), Anne (baptised 28 September 1571 – buried 4 April 1579, Richard (baptised 11 March 1574 – buried 4 February 1613) and Edmund (baptised 3 May 1580 – buried London, 31 December 1607).

John fell on hard times in the late 1570s that would last until the early 1590s. In 1575, John decided to, or was made to, withdraw from public life in Stratford. He had been excused levies that he was supposed to pay by supportive townsmen and business associates and they kept his name on the rolls for a decade, perhaps hoping that in that time he would be able to return to public life and recover his financial situation, but he never did so. He is mentioned in the local records once more in 1597 when he sold some property to George Badger, a draper. John Shakespeare was buried 8 September 1601.

220. Edward Elgar

Sir Edward William Elgar, First Baronet, 2 June 1857 – 23 February 1934, was an English composer, many of whose works have entered the British and International classical concert repertoire.

Among his best known compositions are orchestral works, including the Enigma Variations, the Pomp and Circumstance Marches, concertos for violin and cello and two symphonies. He also composed choral works, including The Dream of Gerontius, chamber music and songs.

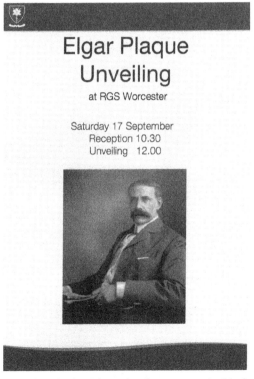

Elgar Plaque Unveiling
at RGS Worcester

Saturday 17 September
Reception 10.30
Unveiling   12.00

Invitation to the unveiling of a plaque at Joan's old school, Alice Ottley School, Worcester.

Much to Joan's astonishment, when she was invited to her old school, the Alice Ottley School in Worcester, she found that he had been a music master there, rising to Head of Music at the school. In his early years, his father had a music shop in Pershore and as a child, Edward taught himself to play every instrument in the shop without any tuition. In the summer of 2016, Joan went back to her old school, where the Elgar Society had arranged to have a plaque in his memory, mounted on the school gates.

Lightning Source UK Ltd.
Milton Keynes UK
UKOW04f0136291017
311820UK00001B/10/P